# Women at War

# Women at War

Drawn and overheard by
Phyllis Pearsall

Ashgate Editions

First published in 1990 by
Ashgate Editions
Gower House, Croft Road, Aldershot, Hants GU11 3NR

Copyright © 1990 Phyllis Pearsall

ISBN 0-85967-847-4

British Library Cataloguing in Publication Data is available

Acknowledgements
The author and publishers would like to thank all those owners who
have given permission for drawings to be reproduced in this volume,
and in particular the Museum of London for the drawings from their
collection reproduced on pages 34, 44, 52, 62, 64 and 66.

Produced for the publishers by
John Taylor Book Ventures, Hatfield
Typeset by Nene Phototypesetters Ltd, Northampton
Made and printed in Great Britain by
The Southampton Book Company, Southampton

# Contents

Happy in this, she is not yet so old
But she may learn; happier than this,
She is not bred so dull but she can learn.

*Merchant of Venice*, Act III, Scene 2

Sewing for victory

# Foreword

Who would expect a book about war – any war – to be heartwarming? Yet that is exactly what Phyllis Pearsall achieves in *Women at War*, for she portrays, along with the horror, the comradeship and the commitment to the common cause that the 1939–1945 war revealed in all spheres, in all walks of life. One comment reported by Mrs Pearsall, from an elderly lady at a sewing party, making a patchwork rug out of tailors' patterns, sums up the tone of the book: 'There's one good thing about this war. Everyone can help in it. Even us old 'uns.'

But *Women at War* is not sentimental. Phyllis Pearsall could never be that. She has the sensitive ear for words that make a fine writer, but she also has the sharp eye of the draughtsman and the compulsion of the map-maker to be 100 per cent accurate. Few women of our time have been more variously gifted and I wish that one or two of her beautiful watercolours could also have adorned this book.

For quite a long period during the war Mrs Pearsall was a licensed observer, visiting the ATS, the WRNS, the WAAF, the munitions factories and the Land Army, to portray with her skilful pen what life was like for the 'service women'. This did not protect her from danger any more than most of us at home were protected. I remember crouching down under the kitchen sink as a bomb whistled down – just as Mrs Pearsall remembers flinging herself to the floor of a WRNS shelter which rocked with the blast while a cascade of rubble was hurled down the stairs. When she emerged she saw a 24-feet deep crater within 15 yards of her. My experience was as shaking, in a different way. Minutes before the whistle and the crash of the bomb my husband had set off for work. It was an agonised minute or two before I heard him return through the slightly damaged front door, shaken but unhurt.

For most older readers *Women at War* will recall similar memories, and how for years after the war ended the wail of a siren made them catch their breath in fear, even if it was only the signal to factory workers that their shift had ended. And every woman whose husband was in the Forces will be moved by this sentence: 'They could confide their torn hearts to nobody, because the only person who could comfort them was the person they were missing so intensely.' For some of us the need to rely solely on our own courage lasted for two, three, or even four years.

What saved us, of course, as Mrs Pearsall makes so shiningly clear, was having something to *do* that took priority over everything else, especially if it contributed to the war effort. As one munitions worker put it: 'By the time Dunkirk arrived we had hundreds of girls in the works and every one of them gave up their Sundays and half days and got down to turning out the stuff for the boys. Never mind about the shopping. We went to it.'

When courage was needed courage there was. It could have been as comparatively trivial as that of the Land Girl who, her friend said, before joining up would have jumped a hedge in terror at the sight of a cow, but after her training would cheerfully lead a bull about. Or as utterly heroic as the courage of a woman crouching under some falling masonry who refused a morphia injection even when urged to change her mind because 'she was suffering needlessly'. 'Not needlessly,' said the woman, 'I am holding up a girder with my full strength and if you give me morphia and I lose consciousness I won't be able to protect my child from it.'

Such stories are not the sole reason why one hopes that not only the veterans of World Wars I and II will read this book but much younger women. Most books about war are by, for, and about men. This book is entirely about the attitudes as well as the experiences of women ... the women in the WAAF who still delighted in painting their nails and those who grumbled about having to wear tin hats because they affected their hair waves, as well as those who after a night-long blitz never turned up late for work next morning. Or the women in the Lancashire ordnance factory who, having worked for years in the Lancashire cotton mills could chat away together while never pausing for a moment in the complicated operation of preparing fuses. Above their heads was a notice 'Every fuse you make kills one German.' Underneath someone had written 'Or makes an Italian run.' Or the nurse whose reaction to the sufferings of her patients was a deep, dark anger. 'Only people who have no pride in being human can start smashing women and children to pieces as if they were of no account. Having to look after cripples, mangled and wounded people who might be happily leading normal lives, makes me very bitter.'

But to me one of the most memorable quotations in the book is from an expectant mother: 'We'll want some decent people in the world when this is over.' Don't we still need 'some decent people'? – people with the sort of commitment to the common good that so many of the women who figure in this book had? Surely it cannot need another war to make a majority of our fellow citizens care not only for those who suffer poverty, injustice, homelessness, etc, but about making a better, less selfish, less greedy life for us all?

Mary Stott

Ordnance factory

TURKEY 10 TIMES MORE CONFIDENT OF BRITAIN'S VICTORY

EUROPE LOST TO HITLER SAYS U.S.A

Conflicting reports

# Preface

Now put your shields before your
hearts, and fight with hearts more
proof than shields.

*Coriolanus*, Act I, Scene 4

When the British Isles were under threat from invasion, and
pillboxes and tank-traps were rapidly built, when all signs
showing the names of towns and villages were obliterated and
beaches were mined and obstructions put in fields to hinder
airborne landings, and when the Home Guard (originally
called the LDV, the Local Defence Volunteers) was formed,
many women had a pitchfork behind the door or a heavy
frying-pan at the ready to deal with any invading Germans,
just as Greek women delayed the Italian advance during the
first weeks of November 1940 by rolling rocks on to them
from the mountain tops.

The production of munitions, or the relieving of men from
clerical, technical or catering duties, may not have given as
much personal satisfaction as the thought of bashing Germans
on the head, but in the long run the work that women did in
the factories and fields, in service camps and hospitals, in the
fire and ambulance services, and in the nurseries, in canteens
and in relieving hardship was of the greatest value to the war
effort.

It was the work of women at war – in uniform, at the
bench, being trained or performing a variety of skills – which I
was given permission to record in the early 1940s. This book
is illustrated with some of my drawings made at that time,
and the text attempts to capture the humour and spirit of the
women who contributed so much to the defeat of Hitler and
Fascism and ensured that we retained the freedom which we
all enjoy today.

Phyllis Pearsall
February 1990

# 1
# The ATS

The ATS recruiting office was not quite what I had imagined. Why, I don't know. I had expected to find formality here if anywhere, but the young officer wrestling with the telephone was as human as any other exasperated woman with housekeeping problems. The flowers gaily arranged on the desk added to the illusion.

'You see, we can't open the new camp until we get the sheets,' she was repeating with bitter patience for the fourth time. 'Yes, I know we had them, but a bomb ... bomb; B for Bertie ... yes that's right, bomb. One would think you had never heard of the things. Well, a bomb fell on the stores.' Then after a pause, during which I could hear only the crackle of her interlocutor's voice, 'We thought of that too, but if they sleep in blankets now without sheets, the blankets will have to be washed when the sheets arrive and then they'll only have sheets and no blankets. You'll do your best, won't you? ...' She put the receiver down.

'I'm so sorry,' she said to a new recruit, who had been waiting at the door, and with a charming smile began to interview her.

'Are you married?' she asked after disposing of a number of other questions.

'No, miss,' said the young woman, as she had not yet learnt the regulations that officers should be addressed as 'ma'am'.

'Have you dependants?'

She blushed with an air of 'and me a respectable young woman!', and answered, 'No, of course not. And do I have to undress?'

'Yes.'

'Ooooo!'

The next applicant, a tall, sloppy girl was shown in.

'Have you worked before?'

'Yes.'

'What at?'

Silence.

'Do you know shorthand and typing or cooking?'

'Yes.' The recruiting officer had not been particularly impressed by this girl, but, now taking it for granted that the 'yes' referred to all three accomplishments, she became almost enthusiastic.

'Good, that's what we need. By the way, what's your speed?'

'Speed?' asked the would-be recruit looking stupider than ever. The officer's enthusiasm waned.

'Are you interested in clerical work or cooking?' she asked wearily.

'May I ask my mother?'

She returned a few moments later with an elderly, white-

Recruiting office

Lecture hall

haired woman who gave the impression that *she* was interviewing the ATS, not the ATS her daughter.

'What I want to know,' said the mother, 'is whether the girls are well supervised when they join the ATS. I think it's much wiser for young girls, don't you, to be well supervised. I mean not allowed out after nine in the evenings and kept apart from the men.'

'Is she interested in clerical work or cooking?' asked the recruiting officer, Lt Potter, reverting to the point she had reached before the mother's arrival.

'I beg your pardon?'

'I mean what can she do?' Silence. 'And what will she want to be trained at before she is sent off to join a unit?'

'I don't think she could be properly looked after; not really looked after, if you know what I mean, not if she is sent off,' said her mother. 'You see when Myrtle was in the Wrens . . .'

The girl bit her lip in anger. 'I knew you'd mess everything up, Mum!'

'Oh, so you were in the WRNS,' said Lt Potter, all interest gone from her voice. 'What made you leave it?'

'I left on compassionate grounds,' replied the girl slickly.

'I'm afraid in that case I'll have to see your discharge papers and look into the matter. We won't arrange about a medical just yet, and I advise you to think things over for a week or so!'

Several more applicants were interviewed and a number of them had had satisfactory experience at cooking, catering, or secretarial work. They were sent off almost immediately for their medical examination, so that they could be put to work (or sent for training if the need for ATS was not too urgent) with the least possible delay. There was, however, quite a commotion as the last applicant for the morning came in with a whirl of talk.

'Of course, miss, I'm a qualified nurse. I nursed during the last war.'

'If you're a nurse, I'm afraid we can't enrol you in the ATS,' began Lt Potter. 'The Ministry of Labour . . .'

'They wanted me to nurse again; I'll show you a letter. I must do something, but there's my husband, he's a neurasthenic so I can't go off to nurse. It means one must pack up everything and go. Do you see my point of view?'

'The ATS wouldn't suit you either,' murmured the officer, unable to stem this avalanche of words.

'Thank you very much, miss; you see I live here . . .'

'You would have to move . . .'

'But I've told you I can't move.' An impasse had been reached.

'If you join the ATS,' said Lt Potter at last, quoting the applicant, 'it would mean you must pack up everything and go.'

'Thank you very much, miss. As long as you see my point of view. So I'll be off then . . .'

\*       \*       \*

'Delighted to see you!' said an extremely smart officer who was wearing a blue band over the shoulder of her immaculate uniform, a band which matched her eyes too well to have been accidental. 'But of course we Orderly Officers always get any

Drill competition

rotten jobs going. Only Orderly Officer once a fortnight, thank goodness! Bit of a nuisance you should come today to draw us, as it's kit inspection this morning and drill competition this afternoon. My company's won the general knowledge and we'll win the other two!'

She was leading me through lovely parkland surrounding a large pseudo-Gothic country mansion. The sun was shining, birds singing, and the recruits, who passed us from time to time on their way to work, appeared in the spaciousness of the landscape like little figures busily hurrying through an eighteenth-century colour print. Some were in pairs carrying dustbins to or from their huts; others were on their way to lectures, while many were joining the group gathered on a sloping lawn which ran down to the lake. Trees of all kinds grew near its banks and I saw below me the small figure of a recruit leaning her back against a tree trunk and writing a letter.

'Idyllic!' I said to the Orderly Officer, as she smilingly turned to address the group on the lawn: 'Just one more practice before the drill competition!' The recruits laughed. They liked their hearty officer and were happy to sacrifice their few moments of leisure in order to please her. In any case they were proud of their company, though ignorant of its existence only three weeks ago.

'Company fall in!' The smile disappeared from the officer's face, 'By the right, march!'

'Heads up, shoulders back and stomachs in!' roared the officer. There was a marked improvement of what had already seemed to me perfect. My standards rose.

'And that applies to you too!' shouted the officer to a recruit who, confusing the order, marched with stomach out and shoulders forward.

Then, to the whole company:

'Do you call that marching? You're worse than the new batch of recruits who've only been here a week!'

The company, stunned by this insult, wavered for a moment. Then they moved forward as one person. Their previous bearing, which had seemed perfect to me, was shamed.

A young, fair-haired officer, with a slight slouch compared to the performing Amazons, nodded towards the Orderly Officer:

'Munro's company always wins the drill competition. And mine's always last. We have about five hundred recruits in each batch and form them into three companies.'

'What a lovely place for the girls to be trained in,' I said.

'It makes all the difference to their health,' she replied. 'They mostly arrive here looking very pale and thin and look at them now!' They were marching round, cheeks a bright pink, eyes sparkling, and none of them unhealthily thin.

'If they started as thin as you say,' I said, 'how is it their uniforms fit so well?'

'They don't get their uniforms until the end of the second week, though not for that reason. During the first week of training we give the recruits a harder time than they will ever get on service, so that those who can't take it can leave. Very few can't take it.'

Kitting out

Captain Munro had dismissed her company and several other officers strolled out of their Mess and joined us.

'If we don't send the girls out drilling well, what use are we?' asked Captain Munro.

'If we don't send them out doing accurate work,' said the clerical instructor, 'what use are we?'

'If we don't send them out cooking good meals,' said the cooking instructor, 'what use are we?'

And each one called her students out of the company and went off with them to the lecture halls or to the huts for practical work, and the students themselves all went eagerly for I had noticed that these lessons were like those given in civilian training colleges. There was no barrack-room manner; the girls were treated as individuals.

'You see,' said the PT instructor, following the line of thought of our conversation about drilling, 'we are sent girls and women of all ages and from all over the place and can spend only three weeks on creating some kind of basis common to them all on which their army life can be built. Uniform is a symbol of that new basis. We have to give substance to it, and drill seems the quickest way of producing a feeling of being part of a whole and responsible to and for that whole. Quite a proportion of the younger girls we get have never done any work, have been spoilt by their parents and have moaned about feeling bored. Drill disperses that moodiness; the girls become alert, unselfconscious and feel of some use.'

A number of recruits who had been waiting about became restless, and Captain Munro, who had already dismissed her company and had been standing beside me for most of this monologue asked the PT instructor 'to get on with it'. The class started with folk dancing.

Captain Munro, whose face had gone blank during the so obviously unnecessary justification of drill, now regained her animation and excused her colleague to me: '. . . but she's very good at PT though'.

'Knickers, suspender belt . . . what's that! The mackintosh doesn't fit? Take it upstairs to the tailoress tomorrow.'

'But I'm leaving tomorrow.'

'You can't be, if you're getting your uniform today.'

'I'm not. It's just that I found the mackintosh didn't fit.'

'You've no right to the knickers and suspender belt then. What do you mean by taking them?'

'But I didn't. You pushed them into my hands.'

'Don't argue. And take your mackintosh to the tailoress and ask her to alter it. Tell her you are leaving tomorrow. And don't forget to be at the kit inspection in ten minutes.'

The sergeant turned her attention to a recruit who was walking with one shoe on and an anxious expression on her face. 'If those shoes don't fit try on another pair. Or if it's your foot, there's a foot inspection on the Parade Ground now.'

'Yes, ma'am.'

Captain Munro approached the sergeant. 'Could you hand over to somebody else?' she requested. 'I want you to make sure our company will win the kit inspection.'

The tailoress

'Yes, ma'am.'

'You're something of a martinet,' I said to the sergeant as we walked between trees to No. 3 hut.

'A wot?'

'You like discipline,' I explained.

'Well, it's like this. They give it to me when I come so I give it to them when they come. They like it.'

She thought back to her feelings as a recruit: 'I'd done a bit of hard work in my life. Things wasn't always easy, but when I settled down to my first week here I thought I'd lived like a queen before. What with sweepin' up garbage, I thought I'd be able to get a job on the Corporation when I was through with this. But it made a new woman of me. Work never killed anyone.'

We entered No. 3 Hut. About 20 recruits in uniform jumped to attention and stood in front of their beds. The beds were not made in the usual civilian manner, but the blankets had been folded round the sheets and round each other looking like a flattened jam roll. Behind this on the mattress, the knickers, shoes, brushes and combs etc., were displayed.

'That's the way girls,' said the sergeant genially. 'If you jump to it like that when our commandant comes, everything'll be hunky-dory.' A crunch on the gravel outside gave the warning. This time the jump to attention was even brisker.

'Stand easy,' said the commandant, as she began the rounds. But each recruit, as the officer reached her, jumped to attention, only to relax when her kit had been inspected.

'We spent two hours scrubbing the floor this morning,' one of the recruits whispered to me. 'Doesn't it look a treat?' It did.

This was the last hut to be visited. The others of Munro's company had been equally perfect. So her second competition was won.

The officers gathered on the pink steps leading down to the sloping lawn. The newer recruits, who had been given half an hour of freedom from their intensive training in whatever branch of work they were to do, were already sitting on the grass banks further along; whilst opposite, amongst the trees in the longer grass, were the recruits who were to take part in the drill competition.

'I hope you don't think us too military,' the commandant said to me, as we surveyed this eighteenth-century scene. 'When I was at my previous post there was almost no time for drill, and it's like that on all active posts. Here we drill once a week so that the women keep smart; and of course, it gives them air and exercise. We don't always have to parade at inspections now either, as whoever's inspecting usually prefers to see us at our work. The work after all is our raison d'être and we don't lose sight of that. I'm always rather surprised that the recruits are so keen on drill – but I believe it makes a kind of break between the responsibilities of their private lives and the greater though shared responsibility of helping actively to win the war. We're pleased that at last we've time to train, because at first, and even now in some

Stand by your beds!

districts, many simply had to be recruited locally to go straight into work.'

The bugles sounded. The commanding officer took her place on the steps and the drill competition began.

The PT instructor called on her company to fall in. The recruits of the other two companies could be seen criticising with a professional eye. The newer recruits watched with growing partisanship the company to which they had been appointed.

The second company's turn came along and finally Munro's. She took off her blue band and put it over the shoulder of another officer for her to serve temporarily as Orderly Officer, and strode out to her company.

Her martial voice as she issued orders rang out in full clarity and precision.

There was no question about it. Her company won. She congratulated her sergeant and thanked her company. She then very correctly condoled with her competitors and praised their performance.

When she finally emerged from her admiring audience, I congratulated her.

'Good show!' she said, putting her Orderly Officer ribbon over her shoulder again. 'Now I can give my attention to you.'

# 2
# The WRNS

The galley was enormous: like the inside of an Atlantic liner but with higher ceilings and much lighter, with windows instead of portholes. And what with the pulsating beat of machinery, the shifting of heavy boxes overhead and the sea breezes, combined with the bustle of sailors and the shouting of orders, one might well have been at sea. The numerous men and women, cooks and servers, all in white, had to shout to make themselves heard. Four large cauldrons of milk, custard and boiling soup occupied the centre and had to be stirred with gargantuan ladles. Stoves were arranged down the two long sides of the galley (the word 'kitchen' had been deleted from my vocabulary by the Wrens) and gave off such a heat that I felt I was in the stokehold itself.

'It's hot here,' I tried to shout above the noise to a steward as I helped a Wren baste a joint.

'What's not here?' he shouted back, obviously mystified.

I tried again, conscious of it being a gross understatement.

He heard me this time. 'I suppose it is,' he admitted as if he had noticed it for the first time.

'It's just like being on a ship,' I said.

'I don't know about that. You imagine doing all the work that's being done here, with a heavy roll juggling with you and everything else.'

'I'd rather not.'

'I suppose it is rather hot,' said the steward, wearying of my apparently repetitious comment. 'Our Wrens can take the heat. We thought at first they'd just be a bally nuisance, but they can work all right and now we don't know what we'd do without them. And they can take the air raids too. But I've got to watch my step with them. Talk about cooks being temperamental, you ought to see some of the flare-ups we get.'

Male cooks and stewards in their white jackets and trousers were lifting heavy crates on to the decks ('tables' to lay people) breaking them open and throwing the contents – long slices of smoked haddock – to the women who rapidly chopped them up and put the now more manageable pieces into big tubs which the men carried below as soon as they were filled.

In a small room opening off the galley, a sailor was feeding potatoes into a peeling machine and, when he had peeled enough, called some of the Wrens over from the haddock to cut out the eyes.

'Come on, Big Bertha,' he shouted at the roundest of the cooks, who had been slicing the haddock with even more energy than the others. 'You can't let me down today.'

'None of your sauce,' Big Bertha shouted back, but after she had attended to one more piece of haddock, she relented and, still wielding her knife, joined the group round the tubs full of

Wrens in the galley

potatoes and water.

'You've got a soft job,' said Big Bertha to the sailor, as she de-eyed the potatoes with incredible speed.

'Soft job having to look after a lot of bloomin' women! I've been torpedoed twice this war, and that was nothing to this.'

Since reaching the galley, I had been amazed at the rapidity and intensity with which everybody worked, but now, suddenly, the really feverish work began. Sailors started to crowd into the galley with their plates and cups. Joints and roast potatoes had to be taken out of the ovens, dished up, carved and served; puddings had to have custard poured over them. More and more sailors arrived, some being served individually, while others held long, deep trays which held as many as twenty plates. The rush lasted a wild half hour, and then the Wrens and stewards and cooks relaxed. There was even a few moments for a chat . . . and a cup of tea.

At the naval barracks the air-raid alarm was only sounded when danger was imminent, so everyone reacted immediately when it went off.

'Come with me,' commanded the chief Wren officer and, followed by her third officer and a number of Wrens, we ran down the stairs to the Parade Ground. Sailors and marines were running everywhere although without a sign of panic, like some great and complicated dance of the Lancers, winding their way to their respective shelters under the Parade Ground.

Two naval officers, who had just been climbing the stairs as we ran down, turned and ran with us to the same shelter.

'Well,' said the taller of the two men to the chief Wren officer as soon as everybody was sitting on the thin slats forming the benches in this concrete shelter, 'I was just coming up to you for that drink.'

The chief Wren turned to me. 'This is our doctor, and I was having a party today before lunch to celebrate the first anniversary of my coming here to work.'

'And not a day absent,' said the doctor.

The guns started firing. Several of the Wrens put their hands over their ears, and the third officer handed them cotton wool. With one exception they took it, put it in their ears and then joined the others playing cards, chatting, letter-writing or knitting. The remaining Wren had already plugged her ears but was obviously frightened.

'By the way,' said the chief officer to the doctor, 'where were you during the morning raid yesterday?'

'At the hospital,' he said. 'We certainly rocked, but there was no damage done. And nobody was injured.' Then he laughed at a recollection: 'Though one of the sentries was blown out of his trousers. He came along to us, thinking he was wounded.'

'You've come to the wrong place,' I said to him, "It's Supplies you want:"'

'Wasn't that a bit unkind?' said the chief officer.

'No, as a matter of fact it was the best thing for him, 'Thank you, sir,' he said, and went off. If we'd shown any sympathy he'd have been in tears. The poor fellow was pretty shaken.'

Take cover!

Suddenly I heard the familiar whistle of a bomb crescendoing as it neared us. Instantly we threw ourselves to the ground. Then came a terrific explosion. The shelter rocked and, with a rushing sound, a heap of rubble, stone and dirt was flung down the stairs by the blast. This had hardly settled when there was another crash and another . . . but not quite so near; finally we could hear bombs dropping further away.

'I hope that didn't get one of the shelters,' said the chief officer as she stood up and tried to brush the white dust from her uniform. Nobody, not even the Wren who had covered her ears at the sound of firing, had uttered a sound while the bombs were crashing.

Then the All Clear sounded.

The danger was over, but as I emerged from the shelter with the others my heart dropped at the sight of a twenty-four feet deep crater within fifteen yards of us.

At the Signalling School a Wren was developing a zinc plate for a one-colour litho machine which did all the printing necessary for this naval station. Another Wren, with a mechanical turn of mind, was on the floor amongst the valves and lesser known parts of a radio set, putting it together. Two Wrens at a desk were drawing a graph of a ship's course. Two other Wrens and a Leading Wren were busy brushing plaster and glass, the result of the raid, off the large instruction sheets they had been working on for days, but within a few minutes they were once more measuring up and lettering.

'Have you done any lettering before?' the Leading Wren asked, mistaking me for a new recruit.

I started to explain that I had only come to look, 'No, I'm . . .'

'Nor had these two,' she said, interrupting me, 'but it didn't take them long to get the hang of it.'

'We'd never done anything like this before,' exclaimed one of the other Wrens, 'and yet we've been able to replace the men altogether in this room.'

'The last man working here went a week ago,' confirmed the Leading Wren proudly. 'You could start stencilling in the lettering here while I get on with this job they're waiting for.'

Unable to resist the urgency in her voice I approached the table, but before I could take hold of the stencil the door flew open and a marine came in to collect a number of finished instruction sheets. Taking advantage of the interruption, I made my escape.

I had been told to report many hours before at HMS *Excellent*, but the air raids had delayed me.

I was put in the charge of a sailor who led me past several ships' figureheads – sadly transplanted from the sea to green lawns – to the officer in charge of the Wrens at this station. She was not in her room but through the half-open door of an adjoining one she could be seen counting table linen while a Leading Wren lifted it out of a large laundry basket.

'Oh,' said the officer on catching sight of me, 'they signalled me to expect you. I'll take you through to the Officer's Mess where you can see our Wren stewards serving tea; you must

Drawing office

Officers' mess, HMS *Excellent*

forgive my leaving you then, but we have all this laundry to check.' Indeed the room was piled high with linen, and long lists awaited checking.

The Officer's Mess was a magnificent room, where tea was being served by Wrens wearing white coats. Beyond, the galley was just like some large kitchen in a hotel and here a chef and several male cooks were assisted by a couple of Wrens.

The main secret work was carried on at HMS *Commander-in-Chief*, and I was rather intimidated when I found myself there in the midst of naval secrets. In the Cypher Room, several officers were busy round a large boardroom table. They were all deep in thought, each with a problem of her own, on which, by the tearing of hair and muttered curses, the result of the war seemed to depend.

Feeling guilty of a certain indiscretion I let my eyes wander to messages and notices pinned on the walls: 'Secret Cypher', I read on one, 'Do not fill wastepaper basket to the brim.'

Another note remarked 'Important' and was equally disappointing. It read, 'Remember to punch holes in the same place!'

Equally unexpected was the bored voice of one of the officers suddenly saying, 'I'd better send this over. The blinking ship's arriving'.

Notices in the Control Room — a room deep in the earth where the switchboard for the whole naval station was in operation — were even more profuse; in fact so showered

under were the Wren and her fellow operator with instructional leaflets they had chosen the only space available on their notice board for a notice of their own: 'Space to Let!'

I was met at the station by a Second Officer whose long-haired dachshund was quickly bundled into the naval car as she, the driver and I settled into it.

We drove at speed along a concrete road in flat, uninteresting country. There were no hedges or ditches on either side, so, as the officer pointed out, if there was an air raid there was nowhere to take cover.

After about ten minutes we reached the large aerodrome. Some planes were taking off, others parked, others landing. Hangers bordered the field along three sides, and army huts occupied the fourth. The concrete road ran along this side, and the car drew up in front of one of the huts.

'We pay no attention to air raid warnings unless our own aerodrome siren goes,' said the officer, 'so when you hear that run as fast as you can to the nearest shelter. And it's best to notice beforehand where the nearest shelter is. If you have time, which you won't have, choose shelters as far away as possible from the hangers. Yesterday we had a bad time. A direct hit on one of them. Two of my girls killed.' She paused and then went on. 'By the way, I'm Mrs Herbert. This is where I live. And this is all the room there is for about sixty girls. They don't sleep here though. I'm the only one to do that. It's no good getting girls sent along here who are unprepared for what they are going to find. There are only

Wren at work

these huts — field kitchens. In fact I needed a cook so badly I had one sent from Greenwich, but her first words were, 'I've never had to work under such conditions,' so I soon sent her away.

'By the way,' she asked me after a pause, 'I suppose the Wrens do a lot of drilling at the barracks?'

'When they have time,' I replied.

'I'm glad they don't do more than that,' she said, 'because I don't drill them here much. There's no time. If there's going to be an inspection one of the men here drills them ready for it.'

Then with her charming modesty, she began to excuse herself, 'You see I'm always rather conscious that my Wrens are quite different from all other Wrens. When war broke out, I called in at the superintendent's, thinking I would just find out if I could be useful in the Wrens, and she said "I must have you right away". I suppose I was stupid, but in the emotion of the moment I signed on and was made an officer. And the next day I was asked to take over these two stations — and that's what I have been doing ever since.

'Of course,' she continued, 'I'd much prefer to be with my husband and daughter; he thinks me mad of course, but as we're stupid enough to be at war with Germany so soon again — how we could have been such fools to let them arm, I don't know — I have to do something about it. I worked right through the last war as a VAD and I am working in this war, but if there's ever another, I won't work in it . . . or rather . . . I suppose I will. You must excuse my going on talking like this, but I never see anybody from outside.

'I shouldn't complain because the girls are very good. They work with all their hearts and the more difficult the work and conditions, the more conscious they are that they themselves are necessary. As they've told me, "working for people who really need us makes all the difference".'

Then as if to explain her good relationship with her Wrens, 'I suppose when one's travelled a bit, it's easier to get on with people. When I was in Malta . . .'

'Did you like Malta?' I interrupted, having noticed that whenever she mentioned Malta her responsibilities seemed to drop from her.

'I loved it,' she said. 'Of course, a lot of people don't. They just give or go to parties, drink and are bored. But I used to go for walks there;' and as if she were re-living some of them, repeated, 'long walks. It's a most beautiful place. I remember one woman asking me what I found to do at Malta, and I said "I go for walks." "Impossible," she said, "You can't walk at Malta, nobody does." "Try it," I advised her. But I did not offer to take her with me as my serenity was so precious. And when I saw her a few days later, she said "How you must have laughed at me believing you really went for walks. I tried it and was worn out for days". She had kept to the streets in the modern part of the town!'

All this time dust was blowing into the hut from the airfield, and the noise of the engines and the whistle of the chill wind blowing across the flat landscape made an ironic accompaniment to the recollections of an individual who was contributing all she could to the war effort in order to preserve the life of

Kitting out the Wrens

peace and tranquillity she loved.

'Before the war became so intense, I remember once going to a Wren officers' meeting,' said Mrs Herbert, tearing herself away from memories of peace. 'And I must say they seemed a sensible lot. No military business. Of course there were one or two of the "We'll show the men" type, but they couldn't do much with the rest of us. They tried to bring in a regulation that officers should never be allowed out except in uniform. "Goodness!" screamed one of the young officers. "Wear uniform on leave; my husband's always said he wouldn't be seen dead with me in uniform. Why, he wouldn't even take me to the movies!"'

I had decided to draw the whole aerodrome with the Wrens moving about at their work amongst the huts, so chose a site on a mound which provided the best view, and began the first outline sketch.

'What are you doing here?' Startled, I looked up and met the fierce gaze of a tall police sergeant whose ginger moustache bristled with zeal.

'Doing a drawing of the aerodrome,' I replied innocently. As I had just started I thought it was the drawing that needed explaining, not my presence.

'What right have you . . .?'

'Oh that,' I replied, and handed him my papers with nonchalance. I knew they were all right; so much trouble had been taken over them. And I went on drawing.

He looked carefully through the wad.

'You haven't a Police Permit!' he barked. It was true, I had not thought of that one. Not with Admiralty papers for a naval station.

'I haven't,' I replied, 'but the commander of the station and the Wren . . .'

'I don't care about them,' said the police sergeant. 'Nobody told me you were expected, and in any case,' he continued, looking at the few lines I had just had time to put down on paper, 'the Admiralty gives you permission to draw Wrens at work. I don't see a Wren in your picture.'

'You're quite right,' I replied. 'I was putting in the aerodrome first,' and added lamely, 'I've only just started . . .'

'Of course you've only just started,' he interrupted me, pride ringing in his voice. 'I am here to guard this camp and no unauthorised person . . .'

I blenched and my hands went clammy despite the cold wind; it seemed a short step from being an 'unauthorised person' to being shot as a spy.

'Perhaps,' I urged rather feebly, 'we could go together and see the commander.'

'I will go and see the commander,' he said. 'Nobody informed me you were expected.'

So, taking my drawing (such as it was), my permits and my Identity Card, the police sergeant left me sitting on my mound. With nothing to explain my presence in wartime on a naval aerodrome I felt more at risk of arrest than when he had interrogated me.

Then to my relief, Mrs Herbert appeared out of the hut and

I went to her.

'I was just coming to fetch you,' she said, 'The commander has sent for us.'

The police sergeant, his moustache still bristling fiercely, was in the office when we went in.

'I am sorry you've had all this trouble', the commander said to me with a smile, 'but it's true that we forgot to inform the police, and I can't see any Wrens in your drawing. To tell you the truth I can't make out anything in the drawing at all.'

I knew it was no use explaining that I had only just started it – people always seem to expect a picture to be a finished product.

Once or twice already the siren had sounded in the village. Now it sounded at the aerodrome.

'Well, Jerry's stopping you getting on with it anyway,' said the commander, pleased to be rid of the responsibility, and we all ran out of the hut. Above me I saw a German bomber diving. I ran as fast as I have ever run. The shelter was not the luxurious affair of the naval barracks. No concrete here and no electric light. A number of men stood on the steps to see what was going on.

'Here comes a packetful,' they suddenly shouted, and tumbled into the shelter. 'Straight for us!'

'Where's Mitsy?' asked Mrs Herbert, who in the hurry and dark had lost sight of her dachshund.

'It's all right, I have her here, ma'am,' replied a Wren out of the gloom.

'I brought some bromides for her yesterday,' said Mrs Herbert to me, 'and they came in very useful. Mitsy didn't need them, but one of my Wrens did.'

The thud and explosion of the bombs gave way to the more exhilarating sound of AA fire.

'Look at that man,' said Mrs Herbert, 'fast asleep. How that would annoy Hitler! He always sleeps like that until the All Clear.'

'How it would annoy Hitler,' I thought, 'to see all of you working with such passion to destroy him. Sharing danger with the men so unobtrusively that they do not even notice you and, rather than saying that everything will be all right, taking it for granted that a packetful is coming.'

# 3
# The WAAF

'They'll make good wives after the war,' said an RAF sergeant as he sniffed the smell of steak and kidney pudding issuing through the open door of the Cookery School. The several huts which formed it were only distinguishable from the rows and rows of other huts forming this training camp for airmen and airwomen by the multiplicity of stove pipes protruding from the roofs.

Inside the Cookery School several kitchens opened off a central passage and in all of these WAAF NCOs were giving the recruits practical work – the preparation of the mid-day dinner, which they would have to eat themselves.

'What I find difficult,' one of twelve airwomen was saying to another in the pastry room, 'is to know exactly how much water to add.' Proceedings had just been held up by an over-enthusiastic recruit drowning her incipient pie crust in water. While she and the NCO recriminated and then co-operated to try to remedy the damage, the other eleven budding cooks, their sleeves rolled above their elbows, stood behind their pastry boards ready for the next step.

'I don't find anything difficult,' came the boastful response. 'I cooked for twenty people at a time before the war,' and she confidently flicked a bit of lard onto the flour as the order was given.

'I've never cooked before in my life,' said another. 'Not even boiled an egg.'

'Stop talking!' said the NCO. 'And now, the water.'

One recruit, who had for some time proved her inability to cook, was peeling and slicing apples for the others. She was dreaming about her possible future as a post-war chef in some slap-up hotel when she cut her finger.

'Are you going to the dance tonight?' asked the girl who had cooked for twenty, taking advantage of the interruption and turning to her neighbour.

'Rather! Harry's taking me. He isn't half sore at having to do all this training. He reckoned he'd be up in a fighter chasing Jerry the moment he joined up.'

'I thought you'd quarrelled with him.'

'Well, so I did. He asked me to meet him on the south side of the High Street the other night. ' "South side," I said. "How do I know which is the south side, or north or west for that matter?" '

'Just swank, that's men all over. They don't know which it is themselves,' said another airwoman standing near. 'They only say that to show off. It's not even as if the south side was the same all the time; it changes with the sun anyway.'

But Henry's girl was on Henry's side: 'He came and said he was sorry and said an airwoman must know about the points of the compass and explained it ever so nice. And about the difference between a Spitfire and a Hurricane, and he's teaching them all to me gradual.'

'Bet you don't know it.'

'Bet you I do. I'd be ashamed not to.'

'Well tell us then.'

'Stop talking,' said the NCO, 'and put flour on your rolling pins.'

'One of the girls was actually ironing! I couldn't believe my eyes!' The NCO's voice was trembling with rage, but as I did not react with the necessary horror, she calmed down. After all it was not my fault I didn't understand – I was only a civilian! 'There are special days for ironing,' she explained, 'and today is certainly not one of them. And if,' she continued, her voice rising again with indignation, 'they can do things like that, I must continue hut inspection and can't possibly show you the way to the Officers' Mess.' In my search for it in the black-out I had bumped into this NCO in an otherwise deserted camp.

'What are you doing here?' she had asked me, sharply, so that I realised there must be some rule that everybody must be indoors at this hour.

'Looking for the Mess,' I had said.

'Oh, it's you. I thought you were one of the airwomen . . . or even a spy.' By her intonation I gathered an airwoman breaking a rule would have been far more serious than a spy's presence in the camp.

'Perhaps if you're too busy to show me the way, you could tell me how to get there,' I suggested.

'Oh yes, the Mess of course. I had forgotten. Now, you see where we are.' I could not, but I let that pass.

'Well, you go straight on . . .'

'This way or that way?' I interrupted.

'Let me see,' she murmured more or less to herself, then to me: 'It'll be that way. You go to the end to the hockey field. But of course I suppose you don't know where the hockey field is.' I felt profoundly ashamed of my ignorance. 'You go right to the end anyway,' she continued 'and then turn to the right. Oh dear, I suppose I ought to come with you . . . But I really haven't time . . .' She was flapping her arms in distress.

'That's quite all right,' I replied soothingly, 'What do I do when I've turned to the right?'

'You go straight down to the end of that and it's the last hut on the right,' she replied relieved. 'You will see cars outside it and it's bigger than the other huts.'

I followed her directions as best I could, but when I did reach the end of the road to the right and made for the end hut, I stepped into mud up to my ankles. This last hut was no bigger than the others and had no cars outside. I was lost and wet through, for the rain had intensified during my unhappy conversation with the NCO, and I knew if ever I did find the Mess I would be late for dinner. I was almost in tears. Only a wretched, incompetent civilian could have been so stupid.

A door banged. Two airmen came out of one of the huts a little way back. I could not see them, but heard them talking. Running along the concrete path with occasional splashes into

Cookery school

the deep mud at the side, I came up to them and asked the way.

'The Officers' Mess?' said one of them. 'I haven't a clue where it is. All I do know is that it's not along here. You'd better go back to the crossroads and ask someone there.' The rain had changed to sleet.

At the crossroads I bumped into a figure.

'Who's that?' it asked, with the now familiar voice I was blaming for my troubles.

'Oh it's you again,' it said. 'You don't mean to say you haven't found the Mess?'

I felt incredibly guilty.

'Well, when I reached the bottom of the road you told me to take,' I excused myself lamely, 'an airman told me it wasn't there and that I'd better come up this way.'

'How stupid of him,' she said.

'I went straight on, where you told me,' I continued, 'and then to my right, as you told me, and straight down . . .'

'To the right!' she interrupted. 'I should have said to the left, but I was thinking I was coming the other way, when it would have been the right . . .'

I ignored puddles now, I was too wet to care, and ran as fast as I could until I reached the warmth and comfort of the Mess.

In this new camp the WAAF officers were sharing the RAF's Mess until their own was completed, but they sat at separate tables. They had their own sitting room where a coal fire was blazing and the daily papers were spread out on a sidetable.

'Have you heard the terrible news?' the section officer suddenly asked us as we were having our coffee. My heart jumped. I had not had time to read the papers. But I need not have worried. News at a training camp means service news.

'Jenkins has been posted to another station.'

'Oh no!' groaned the officers.

'But she can't go!' said the cookery instructor. 'They'll never look after her properly anywhere else.'

'And they will get so annoyed with her, whereas we love her little ways,' said the section officer. 'In fact she is so conscientious I find her invaluable for odd jobs I want doing. She's really a wonderful person when you come to think of it. All her life spent in a home with servants to look after her and then suddenly at her age to join up and live in huts and scrub the floors. Isn't it too awful to think of her at another station!'

'They're sure to speak sharply to her, and that always muddles her,' said another officer.

Light dawned on me. I told them about being misdirected to the Mess.

'That's right. That's Jenkins,' said the section officer, beaming with pleasure. 'Don't you think she's a sweetie?'

'You know, Fellowes, that three hundred new recruits are arriving tonight?' the section officer asked a junior officer, a pretty girl of 21 whom I had noticed about the camp, distinguished from some of the others by her air of diffidence and her tranquil nature.

'Yes, ma'am.'

Separate tables

'What are you going to do about their supper?'

'I thought the only thing to do, ma'am, was to have it put into the ovens and kept hot. I didn't think I would keep Sergeant Lacey up again as one never knows what time they'll arrive. It was two o'clock in the morning last time.'

'Somebody will have to be there to greet them, give them a hot meal, show them to their beds and so on,' said the section officer, who had a pleasant way of discussing matters with her subordinates instead of giving orders.

'Yes, ma'am, I'll be there.'

'Good,' and then turning to me she said, 'It's very noticeable that a lot of girls join the WAAF because of our blue uniform. In fact,' she added with a smile, for she was a blonde herself, 'we seem to recruit a preponderance of blondes. And they also join because they hear from their friends that they'll have a good time. When they arrive here and find they have to live in this enormous camp entirely comprised of army huts, their hearts sink. But soon things improve. They're drilled and find they feel better in their uniforms for it; they make friends with one another and with the airmen; they become interested in cooking (and soon we'll be equipped for training in many other branches of the work which we are gradually taking over from the men), and when they find they can actually produce food that they and other airwomen can eat and enjoy, they become airwomen heart and soul. Most of them, of course, think they want to be off and working at a fighter, bomber or barrage balloon station, but they are nearly always sorry when the time comes for them to go.'

I had seen a batch of them early one morning in a fine mist lining up near the road, each one with a haversack and a small suit-case waiting for lorries to fetch them away. A few left the line to join some airmen who had got up early to say goodbye to their girls, and even a few tears were shed. Then the lorries had driven up – haversacks were flung into a trailer and with cries of 'Goodbye Serg.,' 'Goodbye Corp.,' and many hand waves to their instructors who had come to supervise their departure and wish them luck, they were off to the war.

'It's nice to have spent an hour or so with a civilian,' said the young officer as she accompanied me from the Mess to the main road in the dark. Her shyness seemed less painful when she couldn't be seen. 'It's not that I don't like the Air Force; don't think that for a minute. But I joined up because I wanted to help win this frightful war. I hate the war and I'll be happy to return to civil life when it's all over, whereas I feel sometimes that so many people here are enjoying the service for the sake of the service and do not realise the implications of the war at all. And that's how it should be at a training station, I suppose. It gives a common standard to girls coming from all sorts of homes and lives, and takes their minds off the vast and frightful aspect of the war itself. The biggest dangers and worries become those of disobeying orders or in an absent-minded moment forgetting to salute an officer. So that personal life and experience, so harrowing during a war, become submerged by service details. I don't want to feel that instead of returning to the stage after the war I'll be so

Running repairs

Barrage balloon working party

assimilated by the Air Force that it'll break my heart to leave it. I want to feel that the war is a frightful incident that we are burning all our energy and heart to bring to a victorious end … and that peace is the habitual state of existence.'

We were already nearing the gate to the road, so we stopped a moment in the pouring rain, while she continued: 'I suppose I'm really feeling like this because I'm newly posted to this station, have only just become an officer and fear that I'm not the right person for the job — because it's all still strange to me.'

'Oh,' I said, 'so you're the new officer all the airwomen have been mentioning to me as the officer they like so much.'

'Did they really say that?' Her whole voice lit up. I could not see her face.

'They were telling me they would do anything for you,' I replied truthfully.

'Then I can feel I'm of some use! That does make me feel better!' and we parted.

### Barrage Balloon Station

A balloon was partially inflated inside the hangar and airwomen in navy blue jackets and slacks were scrambling over it to reach some holes in the tissue and mend them. Just when they had successfully negotiated a billow or two the balloon would rear and buck like a frightened whale and shake itself free of them. A fat corporal, however, acted as ballast and succeeded in making a valley in the right place, and the workers settled down to their job. Others slipped inside the balloon through a valve to work there. But I found the inside of an inflated fin in another hangar more intimate. Here the air, with which the RAF corporal filled it from time to time by means of a pump, escaped more quickly and the rubbery wall collapsed about them. 'Give us some more air, Corp!' the girls shouted; and as soon as it was inflated again, 'Stop it, Corp, or we'll bust.' Then when the heaving and rolling of the fin abated, they continued their desultory conversation as they worked.

'WAAFs' mustn't paint their finger nails,' said Elsie, whose nails were a deep crimson.

'You must put all your finger nails in soda,' said another who apparently preferred a rust coloured enamel.

'My husband says coloured nails look like somebody who's just killed a chicken,' said yet another, who favoured 'natural'.

'If you've got a very pale mauve dress and very pale mauve nails,' said Elsie, 'it looks simply super,' and she renewed her efforts on patching up the hole.

'Of course the most chic is black finger nails with a polka dotted frock.' This ideal, expressed by the airwoman whose rust-coloured nails either belied or betrayed it, seemed to settle the question of purely decorative nails.

'White ones in the black out …' she began to suggest an alternative, switching from the chic to the utilitarian.

'You're a one to talk about the black out,' said Elsie.

'Why?' asked rust-coloured.

'Well,' said the sponsor of white finger nails, 'I was at a dance at the hotel last week, and when Elsie and I went up to the Ladies, everything was blacked out. I felt for the light switch and when I found it, turned it on. But instead of the light we expected, we were deluged in water. I had turned on the shower by mistake. Laugh!! How we laughed!' But Elsie had not really left the subject of fashion, and as she started on a new patch for the balloon, she said: 'A green satin bathing dress and green toe nails. Something really outré if you're going to do it at all.'

'They had an awfully pretty fashion in Paris –' said a WAAF who had travelled in the good old days, 'a silk wig the same colour as the dress!'

'Well, I've made myself a barrage balloon skirt,' said a plump airwoman who had made such admirable ballast in the fin. 'So when I go out with Elsie …' (Elsie's slimness was a handicap in this work as the fin frequently lifted her up and threw her off position) 'and everybody laughs at us, I just say "One of us is built for speed and the other for comfort".'

'My balloon girls are wonderful,' said the RAF officer in charge of them. 'They will work all hours to get damaged balloons into use again as quickly as possible. Sometimes they come to us as perforated as the top of a pepper pot, riddled with bullet holes. But that doesn't worry the girls. They settle down to repair each hole as if it were the only one, and won't stop until the balloon is air-worthy again. And when we are blitzed,' he continued, 'and my girls go out to the village to sleep, they never come in late to work. There's just one thing they do grumble about. That's their tin hats. They say it spoils their waves!'

## Fighter Station (Biggin Hill)

'Just popped in to say I won't want the new kit after all. We're not being sent overseas. My, am I sore!' A crew member looked in on two of the women in the equipment office which was situated in a corner of a large hangar.

'Poor Charlie,' said the corporal looking up from her endless forms, 'and you were so looking forward to it.'

'I've been looking forward to it for months,' continued Charlie, too upset even to notice sympathy. 'You people just can't know how I wanted to go and have some fun.'

His eyes strayed to a few shirts, socks and handkerchiefs on the window sill. 'Well, you'd better let me have my laundry anyway,' he added despondently, and carried it off.

'Poor Charlie,' reported the WAAF corporal. 'He looks just as bad as I feel.'

'What do you mean, as bad as you feel?' asked the blonde airwoman sitting beside her.

'Well, what do you think I joined the Air Force for if it wasn't to travel?' replied the corporal. 'The moment war broke out, I thought here's my chance and took it, but it wasn't. When all the people from our section were sent to France, I thought I'd be one of them, but oh no, not me.' She had been stabbing at her forms, but now leant back in her chair for a moment. 'I've always wanted to travel. When I was seventeen I went to work at Cook's Travel Bureau but all the travelling I did was in the A.B.C. or tourist leaflets. 'I wonder,' I used to say to myself as I handed over a ticket to some rich person, 'if you really know how wonderful it is to be

Orderly room

travelling!' I daresay I'll have to join the "Sit at Homes" before I get my chance,' and she returned to her book entries.

A very timid flying officer appeared at the glass door. He was wearing his fur-lined jacket and one fur-lined boot.

'Is this the right place to come for a boot?' he asked apologetically.

'Yes sir.'

'I mean, look here, I've lost a boot and haven't the faintest idea where it's got to . . .' he stopped nervously as he stood on one leg.

The corporal made out a form and handed it to him. 'You'll have to take that round to Hangar B, sir,' she said.

'But I've just come from there. They kicked up an awful stink.'

'You went without that form though. You'll find it's all right now.'

The officer took his form and went back to Hangar B.

'You'd never think he'd shot down more than sixteen Nazis,' said the corporal, 'He's not scared of *them*. Only of Equipment!'

'They're a fine lot of boys,' said the blonde: 'and we've seen them in wonderful dog fights. You should have seen us watching them. Of course we were all supposed to take cover, but do you think we could take our eyes off the way our boys were after the Germans? And the boys on the ground each backing their pilot and their plane to do better than the others; standing with clenched fists and jumping up in the air as if to help them. Nobody's as good as the pilot they've looked after.

I never knew one could live so fiercely and be so . . .' She hesitated for the word to express the emotion which was colouring her face, 'I never thought one could be so proud'.

'None of us could bear to leave this station now,' said the corporal, fired into forgetting her nostalgia for travel by her subordinate's enthusiasm. 'They suggested after we'd had a bit of a pasting that we could exchange personnel with a quieter station for three weeks or a month. Only one or two went, and they came back within a week!'

'The worst day we call Bloody Sunday,' continued the airwoman. 'Some Jerries came over and our boys went up to intercept them, but this lot were only a decoy and the real planes, that had come to bomb us, then swept right through the main gateway and up the path as if they'd been dropping in on us for a cup of tea. I was over there at the time, standing on the grass and chatting to some of the boys. We knew we ought to take cover. When the first bomb exploded we threw ourselves flat on our faces and started crawling along on our tummies towards the shelters. We noticed a little chap crouching by a mole hill, as if that would be any protection . . .'

'I was in the shelter at the time . . .' interrupted the corporal in vain.

'. . . and all the time,' continued the blonde reliving her experience, 'our boys at the guns were blazing away at the planes. Two were on a kind of brick tower which collapsed with the blast from one of the bombs. The gun and the chaps fell with it, but they were up in a second and carried their gun over to the NAAFI tea wagon, fixed it on somehow, and went on potting with it, trundling it about after the plane. Then the little fellow behind the mole hill shouted over to us; 'Never thought the NAAFI would bring us tea with this going on!'

'I was in the shelter at the time,' intervened the corporal once again, at last able to tell her story, 'with some of the other girls, and a bomb fell at either end of it, blocking our escape. We knew the boys would pull us out all right; and we didn't know one of us had been pretty badly hurt. She never made a sound or said anything, but just tried to help us clear a way out. She's only just come back from hospital. When the boys saw what had happened to our shelter, they didn't care what Jerry might do to them; they just dug till they had us out.'

There were many airwomen at this station, their work organised from the RAF Orderly Room. A number were doing clerical work, others operating telephones, teleprinters, etc. Some were drivers and these, when on duty, shared a small narrow room with their RAF colleagues; they called the room the 'Rabbit Hutch'.

The wireless blared away in here, and a kettle was usually on the boil on the stove so that a cup of tea could be quickly made for anybody returning from a job of driving.

The most secret work was being done by the plotters some distance away from the aerodrome. No unauthorised person was allowed into the room where the plotters work and they themselves were in a kind of quarantine, as they alone, with the High Command, knew what Air Force action was being planned.

'Even I,' said the section officer, 'cannot go there without special arrangements being made.'

'They've thrown me out for a day or two,' said a Canadian WAAF officer coming into the Mess. 'They said I'd give them all my beastly cold and that I could come and give it to you folks instead. I thought I'd pop in and see how you and your Pole are getting on,' she said to the section officer.

'She's talking of a Polish flying officer,' the section officer explained, 'who the moment he sees me anywhere rushes over and says, 'I love you'. We had him here yesterday for hours when I was working; from time to time I'd look up to find him kneeling by my side, gazing soulfully up at me. 'Go and make love to Miss Hatcher' I said to him, as I saw she wasn't as busy as I was. 'But it's you I love,' and this, mind you, was early in the morning. Of course our English fellows are furious with the Poles — they say it's not fair — they can't think of love all day long. But they haven't anything to say against the Poles when they get up in the air. The other day one went so low over an aerodrome in occupied France to machine gun the Jerries, that he scratched his wing on one of the hangars. They don't care what they do. But when you think of what the Germans are doing to their people in Poland, one can understand it. I know how awful I feel when I hear the bombers going over here to London to blitz the civilians. I don't mind so much when they bomb here. We're proper military objectives. When we join the WAAF we know what to expect and are prepared for it.'

'That's why I came over from Canada,' said the plotter officer, 'but we get a lot of fun as well.'

'After we were blitzed, we relaxed discipline quite a bit,' continued the section officer. 'I think a lot of the girls were going out to dances almost every night after that. There are the airmen, the Guards and then we have a collection of your Canadian soldiers (that took the wind out of the sails of the Guards) and they all give dances. But we're tightening up a bit again now, as the girls must get their proper sleep.'

A Guards officer, tall, thin and beautifully turned out by his batman, his multitude of buttons gleaming, passed by the window.

'It's a treat to see the look those Guards give our boys when they get out of their planes, their fur-collared jackets on anyhow, and a good old slouch as they walk along,' said the Canadian.' I suppose the Guards are all right, but give me our boys any day!'

# 4
# The Ordnance Factory

The fuse factory I visited in Blackburn was fairly new, and I was astounded on arriving at its gates to see how thoroughly it had been camouflaged, not only by colour, but chiefly in its architectural conception, which, with its long, low lines, merged the building into the surrounding hilly landscape. Once inside, the spaciousness and simplicity of the interior dwarfed the rows of machines, making them at first sight fewer than the thousands that I learned were actually there. The women workers, in green overalls, many wearing green caps, were operating them.

'I'll show you over the whole factory myself before you start drawing,' the superintendent said to me. 'Everybody must see you with me, or else you'll be suspected of fifth-column activities! And heaven help you if some of these Lancashire lassies mobbed you. They're a pretty tough lot!'

The girl who had brought me up to the superintendent's office broke in at this point. 'The other day an air raid started just as the buses were bringing the girls to work. It developed right overhead, and the drivers just wouldn't go on. But we really told them off! "Look at us working to get munitions for the troops from 7 in the morning until 7 at night, and you're too soft to drive us to work!" We got them so that they were more frightened of us than of the bombs, I can tell you!'

The superintendent told me that when he had shown me everything, he would hand me over to his forewoman. 'You've no idea how wonderful our girls are,' he said. 'I was told when I started here that they would only be good enough for machines of the simplest sort with only one operation, but in fact they became so good at the elementary ones I'd back them to do any of the jobs in the whole factory.' His eyes sparkled with enthusiasm as he warmed to his theme. 'I'd like you to notice their hands, incidentally. Almost without exception they have beautiful hands, an inheritance from generations of cotton mill workers; each finger seems to have a separate life and usefulness of its own, like that of a pianist.'

As we walked through the shop floor, I was shown how each group of ten machines was under the supervision of a man – a mechanic whose job it was to keep the machines in proper working order. The women had sliding stools to sit on, but most seemed to prefer standing. The mechanics, I was told, were paid a bonus based on a percentage of the women's output as an inducement to efficiency.

'Most of the pay is for piece-work,' explained the superintendent, 'so no payment is made at the end of the first week of work. That's all right for the local people, because they all have savings, but a month ago I had a batch of Londoners up here, and I thought we'd have to help them over the first week.

Dome and body shop

'"We're all right for money," they all told me, when I raised the matter with them. I found that the local girls on the same floors as the newcomers had had a whip-round and helped them out. The girls will never let anybody get away with paying them short for their time, and will kick up the devil of a fuss about every last penny due to them, but they're unbelievably generous at the same time. They had a collection for some of the chaps who were brought back from Dunkirk, and who were hospitalised near here. I was amazed to learn how much they collected. It must have meant every girl going without a pair of new stockings at least. And in addition to the money, they gave fruit, books, sweaters, gloves and all sorts of things.'

On the shop floor where the dome and body of the fuses were cut out, shaped and drilled, the strongest women were chosen to operate the machines. Men were still employed to do the actual roughing-out and whenever using a machine involved repeatedly working overhead controls. 'We can never keep track of who's expecting a family,' said the superintendent, 'so we just keep women away from that kind of operation.'

As we moved in to the area where the drilling processes were being carried out he remarked that it had been found, contrary to expectations, that the women worked better if they were allowed to chat.

The drilling was done to prepare the body of the fuse for the clockwork mechanism that was fabricated elsewhere in the factory. The fuse then had to be filed, sprayed with lacquer and taken to the General Assembly Room.

I met the forewoman of the 'dome and body' room, who took over showing me round. She was checking the numbers of finished fuse bodies. 'Our job in this shop is to turn out as many bodies as we can, and never to keep the General Assembly Section waiting,' she told me.

A passage ran the whole length of the dome and body shop, and it was here that tiny wheels were being stamped out from a long ribbon of copper. They were then machine hammered to ensure absolute flatness. I watched a girl who held one disc under the hammer, whilst pushing away a finished one, setting another ready to put under the hammer and gathering another one all at once, with the virtuosity of a violinist. The resultant thump! thump! of her music, however, eliminated any further comparison.

All the other bays which opened off the side of the passage were devoted to the manufacture of the intricate mechanism of the fuse itself. Tiny wheels were milled in one shop and tested in another. The testing was always done by girls working for a fixed salary rather than piece-work in order to safeguard the conscientious checking of each item.

A further process involved the drilling of numerous different sized holes, some so minute that the machines for that purpose had to receive constant attention for adjustment and maintenance. Looking after the section was another forewoman, who was in charge of several hundred girls. Her masses of jet-black hair and her white overalls differentiated her sharply from the other workers. She took one of the workers' seats as the girl and I watched, and she drilled a

Drilling

number of tiny holes into some of the little wheels. 'This machine is all right now,' she said. She continued to drill a few more at an amazing speed. 'I loved it when I worked on that bench,' she told me. The superintendent had explained to me that the forewomen were all chosen from the machine tool workers: 'I would never get people in from outside who would have no idea of the work they were overseeing,' he had said.

The trigger safety-catch making machines in one of the next bays were very large, and different individual machines were unequal in their production-rates, so that the workers in that bay, instead of being identified with one machine all the time, took it in turns to operate the fastest machine, and so they all had an equal share in the piece-work pay at the end of the week.

The next process could only be done under magnifying glasses. All the girls wore them on their foreheads, secured with a circular wire band. This enabled them to pull the glass down to their eyes at the exact moment the process demanded. They were rivetting burrs, and their movements were so mechanical, and all worked with such concentration, that they might have been drilled by an army sergeant. Part of the rivetting machine was so secret that I had to black it out from my drawing before leaving the factory.

At these benches, particularly, chatter did not seem to interfere with their work, but there was no danger that the women might reveal any war-time secrets to me: the intricacies of what they were doing was not the subject of their conversation.

'I went to that dance last night,' said one of the girls at the far end of the bench.

'I meant to go, but Fred was on night shift,' said another.

'You didn't miss much,' replied the first. 'It was for old people really. Only a bit of proper dancing, but lots of Lancers and Sir Roger de Coverley.'

'Lancers are all right for those that like old-fashioned dances,' said the girl nearest me, whose golden hair was long and beautifully waved.

They chatted without looking at each other and therefore in rather a flat tone, as they spoke just to use their voices and not to produce a reaction in others, and all the time they repeated the same movements, coming back to exactly the same position like clockwork, concentrating hard as they added one more rivetted burr to the growing stock of fuses. And written on the wall was a notice to give them inspiration: 'Every fuse you make kills one German!' under which someone had added, 'Or makes a hundred Italians run!'

All these bays were as long as the General Assembly Room with workers seated at benches along the two sides. The wide space down the centre was intended to allow the passage of goods and people, but it also proved to be the ideal dance floor during the dinner hour when the loud speakers in every room provided the music and the girls could practise 'proper' dancing and enjoy a well-earned break from their vital work.

'When I was ten I went to the cotton mills every Friday to sweep the floor under my grandmother's feet. She wasn't going to lose those few moments of pay if she could help it,' said Hilda, the black-haired forewoman whom I had seen so passionately attached to her drilling machine. I had been 'handed over', as promised, and the forewoman and I were standing talking in the passage between the Dome and Body Room and the other bays. The bell for dinner had just rung and the factory workers streamed past us on their way to the canteen. Most of them took the dinners they had brought from home out of the ovens specially provided for them, but the others ate the good meal cooked in the canteen and sold to them at cost price.

'You see,' continued Hilda, 'I've always worked in the mills. The moment I left school, I went to the mill my family had always worked in and I took to the work as if it had been in my blood. And of course it *was* in my blood and in my hands too. On pay days we'd take our earnings back home and mother would be sitting at the door waiting for us to put our earnings in her lap. Which we all did and still do. Father, my two brothers and myself. When my brothers married they stopped doing it, but now with the war we're all living together again mother takes our pay as before. She hands us out a little pocket money each.'

She talked of these old Lancashire customs, as if there were no incongruity between them and this ultra-modern factory. The same tradition of work and respect for work surviving through the centuries and giving force and productivity to whatever advances in machine technology science might provide.

'When it looked certain there'd be a war,' Hilda continued, 'and this fuse factory started appealing for workers, I told them at home that I wanted to change over into munitions, but they wouldn't hear of it. 'We've all been in the mills and you must stay in the mills,' they said to me. 'If you go into munitions you'll lose your trade and you'll find when peace comes that the new trade you've learnt won't be wanted any more. That's what happened to us after the last war and we won't have it happen to our children!' But when things became difficult at the mills and there wasn't any work to do, I came into munitions. There were only thirteen of us girls to start with and we'd all been on cotton before, so it didn't take us long to get into the way of machines.

'My mother was still against it until Dunkirk, when the boys came back and said that they'd had to retreat because they hadn't the stuff to fight with: "You'll do the munitions now," she said to me, "and your little sister will go straight into them too, and never mind the cotton." We've learnt now that the Government should never have turned people away from munitions after the last war as if they'd have gone on with them, there'd be no war now, or if there had been, it would've been over by now.'

'Hitler wouldn't have dared,' said Iris, a London girl. 'Not if we'd been armed. Mother has a most unhygienic habit of spitting at any photograph of Hitler she sees. You bet we won't let her touch the Sunday papers till we've read them, as they're always full of photos of him.'

But Hilda wasn't to be diverted: 'By the time Dunkirk

The press                    Stamping out copper wire

happened,' she said, 'we had hundreds of girls in the works and everyone of them gave up their Sundays and half days and got down to turning out the stuff for the boys. Never mind about the shopping. We went to it. We'll never let them have us out of the munition factories after the war,' she continued, 'because we'll never be safe from wars unless we keep up war-time production in peace. I'd be happier working in cotton, but it's no longer a matter of how happy one can be; anything not to have this all over again.'

Iris and the other girls agreed. They had listened to Hilda with admiration.

'These girls,' said the works manager coming up to our group, 'have had a hard time here since they were made forewomen. The workers wanted men over them, although they had realised their worth and themselves elected them as shopstewards to fight their battles for them. But we've done our best to back them up and now anyway things seem to be going better.'

'It was quite natural they should resent us,' said Iris. 'Almost a hundred of us put in for the job and only six of us were needed.'

'And what did your mother say when she heard you had the job?' I asked Hilda.

'She said she knew I'd get it, but all the same she was . . . she was . . . elevated!' she replied, and added after a pause, 'but I cried when I heard I'd been chosen.'

'Why?' I asked. 'Because of the responsibility?'

'No, but it meant leaving my machine. I'd got so used to it.

Seemed like working with one hand without it. You'll never believe me, but I think I was lonely for the old thing at first. That's what habit does to you!'

'Your habits in the North,' said Iris, 'are quite different from ours in the South. We're used to going to our offices at definite hours and getting the same salary at the end of the week and if we want anything changed we have to ask our boss.'

'Well, what do you do here?' I asked.

'It's like this,' explained Hilda. 'At the mills we'd each have our own loom to mind, and if we wanted to go shopping one day or have our hair permed or go to a dance or the pictures, we could go; and if we wanted to work all the time, we could work all the time. Nobody to give us orders. That's independence.'

'Talk about independence!' said the works manager, who came from the South of England. 'These girls didn't half give us a time at Christmas; it sounds a tall story but there were two fellows laid out flat on the floor inside ten minutes.'

I looked at Hilda enquiringly.

'We've a custom up here in the cotton mills,' she explained, 'that at Christmas all the girls kiss the fellows and when a fellow's kissed he's got to pay up a shilling or sixpence — it depends what he's earning — and then we buy food and drink with the money for a feast at our benches in the evening. This year we were forbidden to do that here because of holding up production. But the moment clocking-out time came, the girls rushed the men — the superintendent and everything in

Spraying

trousers. Our chaps from the North were all right, but there were two shy lads from Woolwich, and of course when the girls saw they were shy they all made for them and in ten minutes they were as white as death and flat on the floor.'

'We're not used to that kind of thing in the South,' said the works manager, 'though personally I quite liked it.'

'Some girls come up from the South and think they're all wonderful and the North just nothing,' said Hilda.

'That's true,' said Iris, fair-mindedly, for though from the South herself she had married a Lancashire boy now in the RAF. 'It's silly of them I think.'

'Silly! It's worse than silly,' said Hilda. 'I've nothing to say against the South but they're not worth the North.'

'You can hardly say that,' said Iris, becoming partisan under pressure. 'Look how the Londoners have stood up to air raids.'

'I'll give them that,' said Hilda, 'but so does Lancashire, and so would we if we had the chance. But they come up here expecting to find us wearing clogs and going round with shawls on.'

'I have to admit,' said the works manager, with a wink at Iris, 'that I expected that too. You couldn't believe how surprised I was to find you were a lot of glamour girls!'

Green overalls

60

# 5
# A.R.P.

How are ye blind,
Ye treadersdown of cities, ye that cast
Temples to desolation and lay waste
Tombs, the untrodden sanctuaries where lie
The Ancient dead; yourselves so soon to die!

(Anon. Pseudo-Hipponax)

## Air Raid Precautions

Deep under street level and heavily reinforced with concrete and girders, every borough had its Control Room. Here, the moment there was an air-raid warning, every chair was filled by men and women ready to deal with the various aspects of any 'incident' that might arise.

Large-scale maps of the boroughs lined the walls, some for plotting incidents, others to show the possible effect of damage to public utility services – water-mains and sewers, electricity and telephones and gas. Then there was the elaborate compilation, of which Control Rooms were rightly proud, where every street was indexed and given its nearest warden's posts, ambulance and fire stations; routes were shown as to how the streets could be reached by these services should the main route be blocked by bombs. The next few columns on the chart gave its nearest public utility service depot. At the end there was a complete guide to alternative exchange numbers by means of which service stations could be reached on the phone should the usual exchange be put out of action. This 'bible' was created during the months of freedom from air raids which preceded the first blitz. It had proved to be invaluable when the time came.

When bombs began to fall the wardens in the area of the trouble rang the Control Room giving the fullest possible information. Within a minute, the incident was plotted, the nearest ambulance or fire station was informed of its location, its apparent gravity or otherwise, and of any roads blocked on the way to it. When immediate assistance had been sent on its way, the reports on broken gas mains, burst water pipes etc., which had come in from the wardens, ordinary civilians or the firemen on the spot, were acted upon.

Night and day shifts, as in all ARP work, ensured that the necessary people were always on duty.

## Ambulance and Fire Stations

'. . . then we had that troublesome suicide that never came off.' The ambulance drivers on duty that hot summer afternoon were sitting, or rather sprawling, in the sun. They had had almost a year of waiting to deal with air raids but the air raids had not come as yet. Throughout each day and night, a shift of eight or ten girls was on duty. They knew their

Ambulance drivers on call

districts from A to Z and kept their ambulances in perfect order. From time to time the chief officer would stage a mock air raid, sometimes with, sometimes without, a gas attack.

The newspapers began to complain about money being paid out unnecessarily for services which never might be required. The almost hysterical fear, probably due to H. G. Wells' *Shape of Things to Come*, that on the declaration of war Hitler would unleash an annihilating fleet of bombers on this country as he had on Spain during the Civil War, gave way to a growing belief that we would never be bombed. ARP workers became the scapegoats.

And then came the blitz on London. The ambulances rushed to pick up casualties; taxis converted for use as fire engines were driven by AFS (Auxiliary Fire Service) women to the scenes of fire. The organisation worked perfectly; the girls behaved as if they had all their lives been used to horror, violence, death and collapsing buildings. Young girls, who had been practising bandaging each other for months for textbook wounds, found that real blood and bloody clothes prevented them locating the wounds but the urgency of the moment ensured that they did what they could.

'For most of them that first night,' said one of the women who had been in the Spanish Civil War, 'must have been like a torero's first bull fight when, in place of the chair he had been trained to fight against, a real bull charges him.'

'We were so busy, we could not stop to think,' said a good-looking, very slight girl of about twenty-two. 'I think I went out five times with the ambulance that night. I didn't realise I had never seen hurt or dead people before, but the next morning I was sick and nothing has worried me since.'

As we were talking, a new shift came to take over in the Duty Room.

I had expected to find a great difference in the women after all they had gone through, but they were just as inconsequential as ever, and still with a lot of time to kill.

'My turn first tonight,' Lulu said to the station's chief officer as he came in.

'Always squabbling as to who's going out first,' he parried, laughing. 'I must look at my list.'

'Well, it's much worse sitting here than driving our old ambulances,' grumbled Lulu. 'Anyway, if it's a bad night we'll all have to go and that'll be a sell for you.'

'Just wanted to check you were all here,' said the chief officer and left the room.

'I wanted to go to the pictures today,' Joan started to tell whoever was listening. 'As my husband's on night duty too, I thought we could go together. So we got into bed after breakfast and arranged we'd wake up at one and go off to see Deanna Durbin. He woke up first and said, 'As I'm awake now, we'll get up calmly. Put the kettle on!' Then he looked at his watch. It was a quarter past four. So I went shopping instead.'

'First whistle,' Lulu interrupted, 'Won't be long now.'

'I don't think we'll be out tonight, do you?'

'I don't know, my dear. I wouldn't like to prophesy.'

'... Spanish bags,' continued Joan, too intent on her

Message room

shopping venture to be stopped. 'Patent Leather, sort of rolled up, 3s 6d. Being daft I said to the girl had she got a black one. I don't know why I asked for black. And she was snappy so I didn't get it. And I needed a red one anyway. I must have been nuts.'

'Nothing new in that, my dear,' said Lulu.

'I should never have been called out for that drunk last night,' said Louise. 'It was a police job. These War Reserves send for an ambulance so they don't have to bother any more. A thing like that's a police tender job. Started to fight he did, so had to be taken from the back. I'm used to them, that makes a difference. He bit the policeman right through the thumb. I tied a triangle into his mouth, "You can bite on that," I said.'

'I've got to go to court again tomorrow,' said Joan.

'About your black-out?'

'What was it like?'

'The last chap was smiling all the time and saying your Worship this and your Worship that. He was fined £50. That soon got the smile off his face.'

'They'll fine you £50 too,' said Louise, who always sided with law and order, having had experience of courts when she worked for the L.C.C. before the war. 'And they'll say "if you're in uniform you should know better".'

'For the sake of a week, I wouldn't pay £10 let alone £50.'

'The day you go in counts as one day and the day you get out.'

'What do you do when you're in?'

'I don't know. I'm going to find out.'

'Your old man wouldn't let you go in.'

'The siren's not gone yet. I'm off to bed,' said Joan putting a stretcher down on the floor. 'If I go out tonight, I'll go out as if I was going to the North Pole. I'll put everything on I can get hold of.' She put a few rugs on the stretcher, snuggled under them and went off to sleep. Lulu made up a stretcher beside her.

The other stretchers were brought in and soon the seven girls were fast asleep.

The siren went and then a whistle.

All the lights were out and the girls slept on.

A second whistle went. Three ambulances were wanted.

Lulu, Joan and Louise got up and in a moment they were in their coats and waders and running up the passage to their ambulances. They started them up. The male attendants jumped in and, with lights screened for the black-out, the ambulances mounted the ramp and emerged into the street. The moon was shining and clouds were sweeping across it in gusts. Gun-fire could be heard in the distance; the syncopated hum of German planes droned overhead. Suddenly the whole sky was alight. Cascades of fire bombs like the grand finale of a Redeptore firework display in Venice streaked down. A dull red glow started up where some of these had fallen.

'Here's one coming!' said the man.

The ambulance rocked as the bomb exploded, but drove on. There was the crunch of glass as it ran over what remained of the windows of a house nearby.

Gas kit

'A few more like that and we won't be able to get to Lyceum Street,' said Joan. 'I'll step on the gas. Ah, I told you so,' she brought the ambulance to a sudden stop in front of a newly torn up street ahead. A quick turn up a side street – black out or no black out, she knew her way – and the 'incident' was soon reached.

The casualties were bandaged, placed on stretchers and lifted into the ambulance.

A small boy ran to Joan. 'I've lost my sister,' he said. 'Will you help me find her?'

'She's probably been taken away somewhere safely,' Joan answered.

'I know she's there,' said the boy with the conviction of despair. This fear for his sister had in a few moments invested him with an adult's dignity. 'My sister, lady, my sister!'

'Ambulance ready Joan,' said her companion and Joan had to leave the boy.

'What is your name son?' she asked.

'Harry.'

'Well Harry, good luck old man.'

'Can you take me along in that bus of yours dearie?' asked a woman whose face was smeared with blood.

'Do you think you could walk to the first aid post; we're full.'

'I'll try, love.'

'Well if you can't, wait here for us. We'll be back.'

'I didn't know Western Flats had been hit,' said Joan as she and Lulu stood by their ambulances outside the hospital waiting for the stretchers to be brought back for their next trip. Part of the sky was lit up by a raging fire.

'You don't know everything,' came Lulu's undiminished repartee.

When at last the 'All Clear' had gone, the last casualties been fetched, and the girls were sitting in the Duty Room, Joan said rather dreamily during a pause, 'We had a bad do in Lyceum Street; a little boy had lost his sister.'

# 6
# Nurses

Bearing the bandages, water and sponge,
Straight and swift to my wounded I go,
When they lie on the ground after the battle brought in,
Where their priceless blood reddens the grass, the ground
Or to the rows of the hospital tent, or under the roofed
    hospital,
To the long rows of cots up and down each side I return,
To each and all one after another I draw near, not one do I
    miss . . .

(Leaves of Grass, Walt Whitman)

'My darning was somewhat delayed by the blitz,' said a nurse as she threw down a finished pair of black stockings and took up another. She was sitting in the hospital grounds during her four hours off duty. 'I don't really feel I'm doing anything for the war. Nursing is just the same as in peace-time.'

In fact from the moment I had started drawing in the hospital, I realised that nursing, paradoxically enough, was not like the other women's work, created by and existing for war, but was in fact just taking war in its stride. The pioneer days of Florence Nightingale when she herself had to nurse, beg for equipment, order beds, food supplies and so on were far away. More than anything else, nursing seems now like some enormous standing army, so completely organised and

well equipped that training and experience will decide its actions, not circumstances.

'I'm sorry that you've come to draw us when we're down in the basement instead of in our usual wards,' the matron had said in one of the hospitals.

'But that is what I come for,' I said.

'Newspaper men always want photographs of our nurses playing darts with convalescent patients, and so on; I'm always so frightened a photograph like that's going to appear in one of our medical journals. Of course, when they're off duty the nurses can enjoy themselves, but the hospital is never off duty.'

Downstairs, in the basement, some recent casualties from a not too serious bombing raid were being attended to. An operation was in progress in the theatre — which had also been moved to a place of greater safety — and nurses, still wearing masks over their faces, wheeled trolleys laden with dressings into what had formerly been the kitchens.

'Of course,' continued matron, 'we are hardly training any new nurses here at the moment. We send them to our hospital in the country, where they can get our certificate just as if they'd been here. You see, since the blitzes became intermittent here in London, we frequently have periods with very few patients and that would never do for training. As

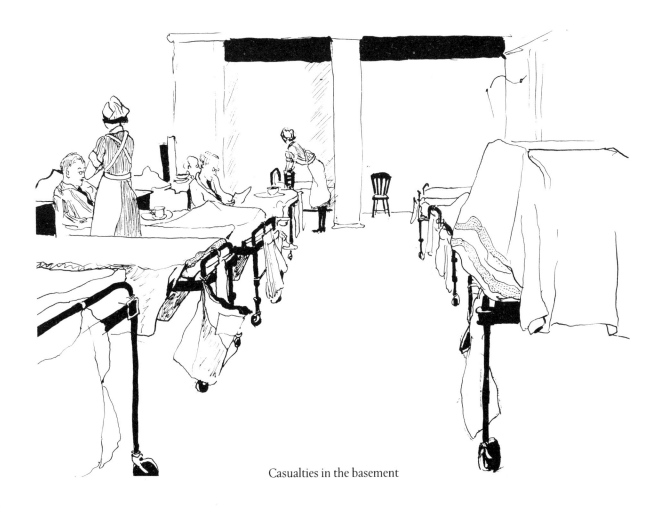

Casualties in the basement

Child casualty

soon as it's possible to move the patients, we send them to the country, so as to have our beds free for the next air raid.'

As she was showing me round, the siren went and, within a few moments, guns roared, enemy planes hummed menacingly overhead and the now familiar noises of an air raid in progress could be heard all around us.

The big doors leading from the road to the casualty station were flung open and it was not long before ambulance attendants were bringing stretcher cases to the casualty station. Some were so grievously hurt that doctors attended to them while still on the ramp; others were treated in the order of the gravity of their wounds. Upstairs on the fifth floor nurses were putting out a fire from an incendiary bomb.

Throughout the night and the next day the stream of casualties did not cease. And it was the same in almost every hospital in the town.

'We all prefer to be working when something big like that happens,' a nurse told me as she sat in the garden following a blitz, 'but it seems such a waste, all this murdering and maiming. I always try to get into the minds of people, but I'm hanged if I can understand the German mentality. Only people who have no pride in being human can start smashing men, women and children to pieces as if they, their lives and families, so rich in themselves, were of no account. It will do them no good. They can't get us down. Look at me for example; to have to look after cripples, mangled and wounded people who might be happily leading normal lives, makes me very bitter.'

Another pair of stockings was finished, but the nurse had more to say: 'Our surgeons are wonderful. You know that this hospital is staffed entirely by women; the electrician and the odd job man being the only two men here. They'll try everything to save peoples' lives. They'll operate again and again. And you see that old man up in the wheel chair on the balcony? Well he's going to be quite all right again, though when he came in it seemed as if there could be no hope. They operated three times on him. I work in the theatre and what does astonish me is to see our women surgeons looking so delicate and frail compared to the terrible casualties they were operating on; and yet last Wednesday they worked something like twenty hours on end without a rest.

'The patients too are so pathetically grateful for anything we do for them, though their chief worry, of course, when they come in or regain consciousness is about their families. Our almoner spends a hectic time trying to find out who belongs to whom, ringing up wardens and other hospitals until everybody is in touch with everybody else. She's no longer looked on as an old witch trying to get as much money out of patients as she can, but as a sort of liaison officer between them and the world outside.

'On that awful Wednesday night, for instance, a little boy who had been brought in was obviously dying. Matron asked him what he would like more than anything else in the world: 'I'll get it for you!' she said.

'"Can I really have anything I want?" he asked. Matron nodded. 'Anything? Then could I really have a . . .' He was so

Feed time

excited at the idea of having such a wonderful thing granted to him that he couldn't get the words out at first. And we wondered what it was going to be: 'Could I really have a lemonade with a straw?' The nurse paused for a moment.

'It was not much to ask, but we hadn't a straw in the building. It was the middle of the night and the blitz was at its worst. Ambulances were bringing in even more casualties. But somehow or another the straw had to be found. The lemonade we had.

'After all sorts of useless attempts, our almoner decided to ring up a chemist at his private address, and told him about it. The chemist got up out of bed, drove several miles to his shop in town and brought the straws round to us. And so Freddy had his lemonade with a straw, and died happy.'

A specialist children's hospital I visited received patients from all over the city so was always full, even though the children were sent to the country the moment their health made the journey possible.

'I've always loved children,' said one of the nurses as she sat on a bench in front of the fire feeding a tiny baby from a bottle. 'Now Lizzy, don't bother Peter. He's having his tea. Come over here and sit beside me.' Lizzy, a lively little girl and the picture of health, did as she was told.

'That's a good girl.' But Lizzy was soon wriggling on the seat and finally her high spirits carried her off round the ward again.

'She's been terribly ill, but has just returned from our convalescent home in the country on her way to North Wales where her family's been evacuated.'

The bottle was empty and the baby was put into its cot, and seemed tinier than ever.

Upstairs, in another ward (a ward adopted by a town in the U.S.A.) the more serious cases were being nursed, and when I was there drawing a baby with a bandaged head a man and woman arrived, the man carrying a little girl in his arms. They looked desperately worried. Their child had meningitis.

'The bed's ready,' said sister, coming up briskly and looking very smart in her starched uniform. 'And don't worry. She'll be all right. Two years ago I'd have been as worried as you are, but now we have a serum that'll cure her.'

In wartime it might be assumed that the nursing of wounded servicemen would be the primary work, but in this war the civilians bore the brunt of the blitz so the bombing raids on our towns and cities was the first experience most of the nurses had of the appalling wounds caused by modern warfare. To make their lives more difficult they often had to attend to the wounded while the hospital themselves were being bombed. Newspapers often carried such announcements as:

**Ten Hospitals Damaged**
It can now be revealed that among places damaged in a recent raid were St. Pancras Hospital, St. Nicholas Hospital, Plumstead, St. Thomas' Hospital, which has already suffered severe bomb damage, St. Mary's Hospital, The City Maternity Hospital, etc., etc.

Hospital laundry

Nursing under such conditions was doubly difficult and yet nurses insisted that they were no more worried by these frightful casualties than by ordinary illness. It was difficult to believe that this was more than courageous self-deception when it sometimes took as long as four hours to clean wounds before an operation could be carried out. Yet according to them it was all in the day's work. The matron told me that 'even young girls of seventeen don't seem upset by it. Nursing is their job and that's all there is to it. I was surprised and pleased myself, though I shouldn't be really as people seem to be able to stand anything for a good reason. Last night I had a call from the demolition men at a block of flats which had had a direct hit. A woman and child were alive, but it would take some hours to get them out. The woman was hurt, could we send a doctor? One of our women doctors drove to the scene and, crouching under some masonry, offered to give the woman a morphia injection. The woman refused. Our doctor managed to crawl under girders and across rubble until she reached the woman, who had a child in her arms. The doctor asked her to change her mind: "You are suffering needlessly" she said to her. "Not needlessly", answered the woman. "I am holding up a girder with my full strength, and if you give me morphia and I lose consciousness, I won't be able to protect my child from it." They were got out alive.'

# 7
# The Land Army

Full many a glorious morning I have seen.

(William Shakespeare, Sonnet XXXIII)

'There's one thing about the country – you either like it or you don't,' said Susan as she weighed a pail of milk. It was half past five in the morning and the cold east wind which swept the countryside penetrated the cowshed where several land girls were busy milking.

Susan took the pail off the hook and went over to the chart on the wall giving the name and daily yield of each cow.

'Strawberry gave two and a half yesterday,' she said to Miriam who was watching her anxiously. 'She can't suddenly have dropped to one and a quarter.'

'Well, how was I to tell whether I'd finished or not?' asked Miriam a little petulantly. After all, she was used to a bell ringing every time she reached the end of a line on her typewriter.

Susan, who was a land girl of some months standing and who had been kept on here to help train others, explained the art of milking once again.

'Why I keep getting girls who don't know anything more about dairy farming than "where are you going to my pretty maid?" I don't know!' and she finished milking Strawberry herself.

It took about two hours to milk all the cows, and then they were driven out of the shed to fields nearby while a small dog, which was also being trained, yapped at their heels as it had been taught, with sudden enthusiastic rushes to the front of the herd which halted them or made them scatter.

The sun had risen now in an almost cloudless sky and an appetising smell of breakfast encouraged the girls to finish their work as quickly as possible, but the milk still had to be pasteurised and bottled and loaded on the waiting lorries. Pails clanged, as they always do on farms, girls called to each other, taps ran noisily, water splashed. Finally the lorries were loaded and roared away, and the dairy, beautifully clean and tidy, could now more or less be left until the afternoon milking when the process would be repeated.

Breakfast! Girls who in towns had hardly gulped down a cup of tea or coffee and ate a piece of toast before dashing off to their offices in the mornings, had different ideas about breakfast now. Two hours of work on just a cup of tea was certainly a better appetiser than a crawl out of bed after a late night out. The colour on their cheeks was not the result of an application of rouge, but the sign of a healthy life in the open air.

These land girls were trained as dairy farmers, general farmers,

Girls on the land

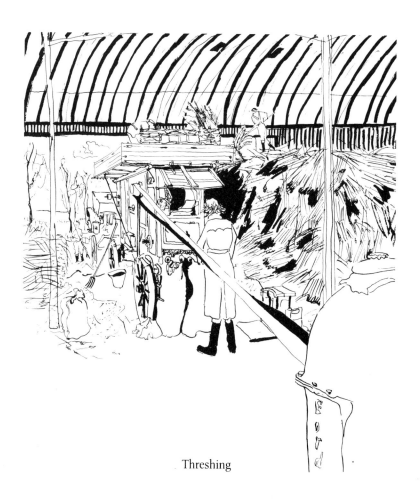

Threshing

or as nursery and market gardeners. On their arrival at this Farm Institute near Winchester they were given a short description of the type of work involved in each category, and then asked to decide what they would like to do.

It was explained that general farming did not demand the same strict routine as dairy farming, as cows had to be milked twice daily, seven days a week. On the other hand general farming involved a varied range of work which had to be undertaken when time, machines and, above all, seasons and weather permitted. 'Of course,' said an instructor, 'it is quite impossible to demonstrate in three weeks of any one part of the year what farming involves season by season, and that is all the time we have before sending them out to farms where they are needed. All I can do,' he continued as we walked towards a cart and horse which had been standing idle for some time, 'is to give these women a general idea of what farming means. Dairy farming and threshing are really the only jobs that have to be done all the year round. The first thing they have to learn is that they'll have to get their hands and overalls dirty, and their hair out of wave. That has robbed England of quite a few farm workers!' he added with a laugh. 'You see, unlike office work, if they are worth having at all they must take an interest in what they are doing. We can give them instructions, but they have to develop these instructions.'

We had just reached the cart. A platinum blonde was lounging gracefully beside the horse, stroking its nose. She had noticed the approach of the handsome instructor.

'Why aren't you stacking up the cart with manure and taking it over to the field, as I told you to?' he asked.

Her eyelashes fluttered.

'Oh but I did. And then I had nothing more to do.'

'I can't be everywhere at once,' said the instructor and, abandoning further argument, said, 'Now back the horse and get the cart right up to the heap.'

Blondie took hold of the reins near the horse's mouth and leant back. The horse instead of backing as it should have done, plunged.

'Why won't anything here ever do what one wants it to?' she cried, hankering after slot machines, buses and other reliable things. 'Look,' she said showing her hands, 'at least I don't mind getting them dirty!'

Threshing was in full swing when we got over to Gordons Farm. A Fordson motor ran the threshing machine. One or two girls were standing high up on the stack of grain inside a long open barn. They fed the thresher from up there while on the ground another land girl, Sheila, hung sacks to catch the grain and, as each sack was filled, weighed it on a machine nearby, made a note of the weight and stacked it for removal.

She did her work with an intensity and economy of movement that singled her out as an integral part of the scene with the sun shining, the trees in full leaf and a warm wind. Her hair blew over her face, her eyes sparkled.

'I love every minute of it,' she said.

At the other end of this ramshackle but efficient machine,

two other girls were collecting the chaff and stacking it on a separate pile.

There was not much talk as the noise of the engine and rattle of the thresher drowned any attempt at conversation. Three terriers, which had been brought down especially to catch the rats that ran out from time to time, were always somewhere else when this happened, sniffing some quite harmless piece of straw to show how keen they were.

The Fordson was stopped, a heavenly silence ensued and Sheila and I were soon walking across the fields towards the farmhouse.

'I used to go to the pictures every evening,' she said, 'and do you know I haven't missed it at all. But some girls miss it terribly. You see, if they're not interested in the work here they're done for. There were some here last week who joined the Land Army for a lark. They thought that life in the country was a cheap return fare to Maidenhead or a bicycle ride to pick bluebells and bring them home dropping over handlebars. They were terribly unhappy. For them, when work is over, life begins. And to find here that the loneliness of the country can only be dispelled by living for it, got them down. I never thought I'd be able to stick it when I first came.'

We had reached the market garden. Its rows of vegetables, greenhouses and frames made a large, neat rectangle cut out of the easy-goingness of the hills around – a sudden concentration on detail separated from its background by neatly clipped hedges.

Inside one of the larger greenhouses the girls were thinning seedlings, their movements deft as they took the small plants, dug a small hole for their roots, scrabbled the earth in round them and pressed it down. When a box was full they filled the next with the loam, beating it down to make a compact soil, and then resumed the transplanting. When half a dozen boxes or so were ready, one of the girls picked up the long necked watering can and showered a fine spray of water over the, by now, drooping seedlings.

I passed through a door into the far warmer tomato and cucumber house where land girls were tying up the plants; appearing and disappearing behind the foliage, crouching, standing upright, looking in fact like exotic figures in some tropical painting by Gauguin.

At about half past two in the afternoon, I saw Susan and Miriam, whom I had seen milking the cows at dawn, being carried across the fields at great speed in a rickety cart drawn by an enthusiastic but diminutive horse. *He* might last for years, but not the cart. Its wheels, almost wrenched from their sockets by years of similar bumping, had developed a double motion lurching in and out at each rotation.

They were on their way to the bail milker, a sort of lean-to shed in the middle of a field where a herd of cows, that remained out of doors all the year round and in any weather, were milked.

But this bail milker was not as simple as a lean-to shed. It had nothing in the large open field to lean against, and was supported by two steel posts instead. It consisted of four compartments connected by a series of rubber tubes to a hut on wheels standing just beside it. This latter contained the pumping machinery and milk churns, instead of the gypsies that its chimney, with the smoke coming from it, might have led one to expect.

The cows, driven from their grazing, were kept outside this Heath Robinson affair until their turn came by a quickly erected fence of steel gates on wheels which leant against each other. Then, let singly into the small enclosure thus formed, they trotted of their own accord straight into one of the empty stalls, where the mechanical milker was attached to them. The milk flowed through the pipes into the churns, automatically recording on a dial the quantity obtained. This done, a trap door shot up in front of the cow, through which she lumbered out into the field.

Susan seemed to be everywhere at once, attaching or detaching the mechanical milker, recording the quantity of milk obtained from each cow on to the chart, and finishing off the milking of each cow before opening the trap door. Miriam watched her spellbound, though from time to time she was summoned to wash the cows or take a hand at the work herself.

But suddenly after a few coughs, the machine stopped altogether, and had to be seen to by the man in charge of it.

'You do work hard, Susan,' said Miriam.

The machine started up again. The cows, impatient at the delay, were mobbing the rickety fence and one broke through it. Miriam shooed her away and shoved and slapped as to the manner born.

'And to think, Miriam, that a week ago,' said Susan, 'you'd have jumped a hedge in terror at the sight of a cow. And now you'll even lead the bull about.'

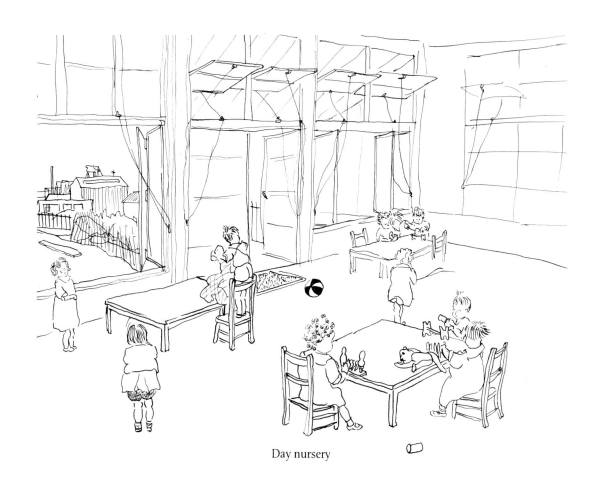

Day nursery

# 8
# The Day Nursery

'Oh Lily can't get here quick enough,' said a mother, as her little girl wrenched herself free and rushed into the day nursery the moment the doors were opened.

'Go away! Go away!' screamed Terence, a boy of two, to his slightly older brother who was trying to drag him out of the pram.

'This is his first day here,' said the mother, unperturbed. A year before she had seen her other son's unwillingness to enter the nursery turn to enthusiasm. 'He's two today, so his Dad and I are going to the pictures to celebrate.'

Another howl from Terence – after all, it was his birthday. But his protests were already giving way to curiosity about the other children, so, relaxing his resistance, he allowed his brother to put him on his feet and pull him along the cement path. He showed boundless interest in every pram, leaf, bit of paper or drain that they passed, so that in whatever direction he was led there were several other directions he would simultaneously (not realising the limitations of the human body) have more eagerly followed. He did his best, and from the one fixed point where his brother's hand held his, twisted, tripped over his feet, flew even for a short distance, and finally, walking back to front up the steps to the nursery, left out one or two, and, dragging his brother after him, fell down.

'Yes,' his mother continued, ignoring the screams which had now become the nursery's responsibility and no longer hers, 'Dad and I have taken the afternoon off, as this will be the first time since Terence was born we've got the chance to go out together.'

The nursery staff had by this time picked Terence up and removed him and his protests indoors, leaving the brother – who up to now had seemed too good to be true – at liberty to pull the hair of a new arrival.

'Bring the children up lovely, they do here, so gentle and patient with them,' said Mrs Hemming, the victim's mother, giving a cuff to her daughter who had inadvertently stepped on her toe. 'And you have to have patience with them don't you.' Mrs Hemming had been evacuated from London with her three children.

'Well, hit him back then,' she shouted at her son who was now howling that wrong had been done to him.

'They'll always fight,' said one of them. 'It's human nature.' There seemed to be a concensus of opinion that standard of behaviour in and out of a day nursery, for both children and others, were two very different matters.

'War to end wars, my eye,' said Alice, a good-looking young mother. She still remembered her school days, though the details were blurred. 'They gave you a regular mouthful of wars at school ... even in the Bible.'

'Of course, what I say is: what always has been always will be,' said Mrs Burgess. She was so old that she had been shelved before the war started, but had now come back into circulation to take and fetch her great grandchild to and from the nursery. 'I remember seven or eight wars,' she said, and, starting to climb the ladder of her memory from the present war, she progressed chronologically backwards through the Great War, the Balkan War, the Russo-Japanese War, the Boer War, the Afghan War, the Franco-German War to the Crimean War.

'You do remember things, Granny,' said Alice, whose school days had left her with no long string of names like that, but with a respect for learning which she now mistook for experience.

'I remember the Crimean War well,' reminisced Mrs Burgess, abandoning the philosophy which had brought her to it. 'I was stitching black beads on to the soldiers' hats. And my youngest grandson, he joined up the other day.'

Wars were really all the same, and she swung from the Crimean to 1940, obliterating any gap. 'Joined up sudden without telling his Dad or his Ma or the man where he works. 'I'll have to tell them all on Saturday' he said to me, 'I like to get things all over at once.' 'Can you cook?' the sergeant said to him. 'Cook. Of course I can!' He'd always liked pottering about in the kitchen, ever since he was a little nipper. 'I won't cook,' he says next, 'if I can't have my pals with me.' 'How many pals have you got?' 'Three.' So they're all cooking together now.'

'What happened when he told his Ma and Pa?' asked Mrs Hemming, who, living a life of drama herself, had a taste for it.

'Told them what?' Mrs Burgess liked to go forward in her thoughts, not back.

'He'd joined up.'

'Who'd joined up?'

Alice thought she had better straighten things out.

'You said your grandson didn't tell his Ma and Pa he'd joined up.'

'I never did!' said Mrs Burgess indignantly. 'He's a good boy and wouldn't do anything underhand.' Obviously it was no good pressing Mrs Burgess further. In any case it was time to get off to work.

Inside the light and airy nursery, the children looked very neat in overalls all of the same cut but of different colours; they sat around tables playing the specially selected games considered by psychologists as pleasant for a child and good for its brain. The hammers for banging pegs into holes were chiefly used on each other's heads, a pastime which may or may not have been good for brains, but in any case afforded great pleasure.

For a small payment of two shillings a week or less or even nothing if conditions warranted, the parents could leave their offspring in this children's paradise.

Rocking horses, slides and other toys and games were sufficiently plentiful for all of them, and a nurse would always be there to intervene whenever a child stronger than the rest tried to throw another off the rocking horse or out of a motor

Honk, honk. Gee up!

Meal time

car or train, and, like some more successful League of Nations, she would give fair-play to the weakest.

At meal times the children helped to lay the table; the smaller ones, those at the hammering-of-pegs age, hindering more than helping. In fact Terence, whose birthday was being so unfairly fêted by his parents, finding he could not unfold the tablecloth and whisk it over the table, climbed on to his chair and tried from higher up. For one moment the cloth rose in the air, but settled almost immediately onto Terence instead of the table, wrapping round him, so that he could no longer see. Terence struggled blindly and fell with his chair on to the fortunately not-too-distant floor. He was rapidly picked up, disentangled, put on his feet again and his tears mopped. Only the sight of food stopped his screams.

After dinner, blinds were drawn and the children put into cots where they slept soundly.

'This is the best time for us,' the matron, who was only twenty-four, whispered to me as we peered over the cot's edge at Terence's falsely angelic face, 'except I suppose when we put them back into their clothes and hand them back to their Mums and Dads.' She laughed at herself. 'Of course,' she added, tucking in another small child, 'I could never do any other work now I've lost my heart to this . . .'

Late arrivals

She cried herself to sleep

# 9
# WVS and other women's services

That wife is best (as prudent men have found)
Who bring for dower a character that's sound.
No marriage portion serves a man instead
To stave Domestick Ruin from his head.
He'll find no shrew to task him, but a friend,
A fellow-worker, faithful to the end.

(Greek Anon)

The spontaneous wish to help, which swept the whole of Britain after Munich, became even more widespread at the outbreak of war, resulting in the formation of voluntary organisations all over the country, or the expansion and adaptation of existing ones. Some were under a central control, others were purely local.

The WVS was formed in 1938 with the primary aim of assisting local authorities with defence work, though, as the need arose it provided a wide range of essential services and contributed magnificently to the war effort. When the war started tens of thousands of London children were evacuated to the country. Most of this great exodus was in the hands of the local authorities vastly helped by members of the WVS. These modern Pied Pipers collected children at different stations or schools and escorted them across the town to Main Line stations where other volunteers took over and accompanied the children to their new homes. Day after day this continued from early morning and through the nights. We in London could hear the roar of the trains at night taking our children to safety.

It was felt that some children could not undertake the whole journey in one, so rest centres for the 'under fives' were prepared where they would spend their first night away from home. At one of these I found the children playing in a large airy room. They seemed quite gay, but within a few minutes matron brought in two new arrivals one of whom, after looking blankly about him, burst into tears.

'There now,' said the matron to the elder of the two. 'Try and comfort your baby brother.' It was all he could do to avoid crying himself. The other children, who at first looked startled when the crying started, continued for a few moments playing as before and then the terrible misery of separation clutched their poor hearts. One after the other they began wailing 'Mummy, mummy', and 'I'll be good mummy, if only you'll let me come back.'

'It's terribly sad,' said matron. 'At first I didn't think the nurses or myself would be able to stand it. But then I went down to the country to see the first batch that had gone through our hands, and found them happy and well. It's the first 48 hours they find so hard. But the one's who do cry, get over it better. The children who just break their hearts in silence remain unhappy far longer.'

But a diversion was made. The children had to be potted. Then they were given their tea and not long after tea they were all tucked up in their cots, with a doll, teddy-bear or panda each, and the blinds drawn. Some clutched the toys, but others just put their head back and howled. Nothing would comfort them.

'There, there,' said the matron to a little girl who was shaking her cot with her sobs. 'Here's a sweetie for a good little girl.' But the sweet was not accepted. She was inconsolable.

Only little Alexander, who arrived after all the other children were in bed, didn't cry. He remained standing in the middle of the room, bewildered but dignified, the label with his name and address pinned to his back.

At the Reception areas, local organisations of women helped to find billets and did their best to settle difficulties that arose. They arranged meals in halls or large rooms for evacuated children and mothers, so as to relieve the women in whose houses they were staying from the perpetual extra work. On washing days, particularly, mid-day dinners were prepared, cooked and served by voluntary women workers.

At one small country town, I saw about sixty children given their dinner in one room. It had to be done in three batches.

A roll call was taken by a voluntary helper, who, not being able to cook, was considered capable of this — but the vitality of our Cockney children persists wherever they are.

'Mary Phillips?'

'Yes?'

'Yes, what?'

'Yes, please.'

'No I mean, don't say "yes", children, say "here!"'

A roar of 'Here! here! here!'

'One at a time, and don't shout.'

Starting spontaneously like soldiers numbering, 'Here, here, here,' travelled from the first to the last table.

'Now will you attend to me . . . Maureen Stanley.'

'Here.'

'That's a good girl.'

'Pinch her,' said a boy at the other table to Maureen's neighbour, who did so.

'Please Miss, they've pinched me.'

'Tell tale. Horrid little tell tale.'

'John White.'

A united yell of 'Second batch.'

'Harry Leadbeater.'

'Second batch.'

'Listen children, don't all say "second batch" together. It's very nice of you to let me know . . .' she had looked up, 'John White! Why did you say you were second batch, when you're here.'

'I didn't.'

'You should have said you were here.'

'They talked too loud.'

'You could have shouted.'

'You told us not to shout, Miss.'

Miss Morrison gave up. She had always held that children should be treated reasonably and never bribed.

'If you don't all answer quickly, there'll be no pudding today.' And she won.

Another great service rendered by the WVS and other volunteer workers was in running canteens: permanent canteens at centres where there was a constant stream of servicemen, such as at Main Line stations, and mobile canteens which could go wherever they were needed at a moment's notice. These women were on duty day and night and drove their huge, clumsy canteens regardless of bombing raids, fires and shrapnel to supply the ARP workers and firemen with hot drinks and food while they worked. When a whole town had been blitzed a fleet of canteens rushed up to feed its population. When aerodromes were being harassed by the enemy, mobile canteens were driven right on to the tarmac and hot drinks given to the pilots, while still in their planes.

Rest Centres for refugees, following the fall of France in 1940, as well as for bombed out people in this country, were also run by voluntary workers, many of whom took over the evening shifts after their day's work. Food was cooked and served to the homeless. Beds were made up. And comfort and loving care provided.

'They are so pathetically grateful for everything we do,' said one of the workers, 'so that one feels guilty at not being bombed out oneself.'

The WVS, YWCA and Salvation Army all took part in organising welfare work. If the members were liable to conscription, they had to work full-time like any paid worker, or else were called up. But a great number of these women had young children, their own and other people's, to look after, the gardening to do ('Digging for Victory'), and their housework, or, having worked for their living all day, gave their services in whatever spare time they had. Sewing parties made blankets and clothes for evacuated and bombed out people; as one old woman said to me as she was making a patchwork rug from tailor's patterns, 'There's one good thing about this war. Everyone can help in it. Even us old 'uns.'

Even before the First World War women who had known nothing of nursing bought books on first aid, asked their relatives 'to hear' them and, as they became more proficient, felt the pulses and bandaged the limbs of long-suffering friends. Many of these women joined the Voluntary Aid Detachments (the VADs) which were recruited by the Red Cross, St John and the Territorial Forces Association, from 1909 onwards, specifically to assist the Territorial Army Medical Services. During the war these volunteers gave a wide variety of assistance both at home and abroad, not only as nursing auxiliaries in military and Red Cross hospitals and convalescent homes but also in many other occupations such as catering and ambulance driving.

Refugees from France

From the start of the last war the nurses were to be seen on duty at ARP posts, on hospital trains and, in fact, wherever their ministrations were needed.

The first blitz on London created over-night a troglodyte population. People fled into underground shelters including, in London, to the deepest of all – the Underground Railway station platforms. No authority could withstand it. The tube stations were quickly filled, and authority had to bow to a *fait accompli*. But it still had to organise it, and while adapting itself to dealing with something it had forbidden and therefore for which it had made no provision, this new underground population needed proper attention.

Quickly the WVS came to the rescue with tea and refreshments, and auxiliary nurses, with probably just one first aid box here and there, spent these first terrible nights of bombing down on the airless, overcrowded platforms – comforting and attending to crying children, to people with sores or colds or other ailments, working all night with insufficient equipment. But as soon as possible life in these shelters was properly organised and new equipment replaced the original single first aid box, mainly with the help of generous aid which arrived from the USA.

It was an heroic task but one for which the Red Cross and St John Ambulance nurses were ideally suited, and their work undoubtedly relieved the distress of tens of thousands of Londoners. But it was only one of the countless examples of the valuable work performed by these nurses during the war.

Many adventurous women who drove cars before the war enrolled in the Motorised Transport Corps (MTC) and other driving units. They were detailed to the services, Government departments and so forth, and often became extremely efficient drivers and motor mechanics.

'You needn't be frightened driving with me now,' one of them said to me, and she was right. Gone were the peace-time days when, while careering along the North Circular Road, she had taken out her powder and lipstick and started to apply them, saying to me, who had never driven in my life, 'Just hold the wheel a second, please.'

It is impossible to include all the different kinds of work undertaken, as the work depended upon the need, but women were always prepared to have a go. In fact, if hospital staff can be compared to a standing army, the voluntary workers might really have been considered as a kind of Home Guard, ready to tackle any problem which might arise in its own locality until, if required, greater resources could be brought up.

As the war progressed, more and more jobs were taken over by women, for instance as railway porters, bus conductors, and Underground personnel. The bus conductresses had the blitz to face out of doors, and girls on the Underground platforms acquired hoarse voices from shouting out the names of stations, but none of them seemed to mind much.

'Talk about laugh!' one of these latter said to a colleague between two trains. 'Fred keeps pretending he's going to have me sent to Cockfosters Station. "Dive bombing they have there, honest," he says to me, "One chap had to lie under a train for hours!" Kidding me that's what he was!'

'If you give me any more of your dive bombing,' I said to him, 'I won't go to Cockfosters.'

A train roared in.

'King's Cross! King's Cross! Hurry along there please — hurry along.'

And those civilians using those trains were mostly office workers in Government Departments, a high proportion of whom were women, and employees of firms whose work was essential to the national war effort. And they were the first to help to put things right if their offices were damaged.

Then there were just the ordinary mothers of families, looking after their children and homes — doing the housekeeping which is 'think, think, think all day long', bringing up the new generation 'because, after all,' as I heard an expectant mother say, 'we'll want some decent people in the world when this is over.'

Most of them (and now I must include all the women in the country) had their men in the fighting services or were, in any case, separated from them. They could confide their torn hearts to nobody because the only person who could comfort them was the person they were missing so intensely. 'Take care of yourself,' their hearts cried out. 'If anything happened to you I don't think I could bear it!' And many of those experiencing all the anxieties of looking after their first-born child (which frequently the father had not yet seen) would say, 'Tommy's got a temperature tonight. I wish you were here. I wonder if I'd be so upset and worried about him if there wasn't an air raid on. I do try to be good dear and not to worry too much, but I do wish you were here!' Instead of leaning on the person they loved they had to lean on their own courage. It did not fail them.

And the same can be said of all the women now veterans of air raids. The spirit of those days was, 'They say we can take it. Well we have to take it. That's all. We wouldn't take it for fun. But we can't have that Hitler and Mussolini messing us up, so what else can we do?'

It was a real privilege to see our women giving the men a hand — and what a hand. They showed so clearly by the passion with which they worked that this war in all its cruel intensity was a fight for the pride and living courage of freedom against the deadly terror of oppression — and worth it!

And to return again to a comparison with the indomitable Greek women, but this time to those of ancient Greece:

Be amazed
At the courage and great strength of a woman.
Look what a fight she makes, her head unflinching,
Her maiden spirit high
Above the struggle:
Fear makes no winter in her heart.

Pindar

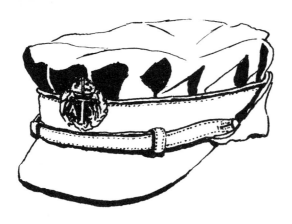